Ellen Harrold

The Aesthetics and Conventions of Medical Art

The Aesthetics and Conventions of Medical Art

An imprint of Boom Publications Ltd
272 Bath Street
Glasgow SCOTLAND
G2 4JR

Boom Graduates and the logo are trademarks of Boom Publications Ltd.

Boom Publications Ltd is a more-than-profit company, dedicating over half our profits to university scholarships for underprivileged students worldwide. In order to offset our carbon footprint, we also pledge to plant a tree for each graduation book commissioned.

The Aesthetics and Conventions of Medical Art
was first published in Great Britain in 2022.

Copyright © Ellen Harrold. Ellen Harrold has asserted her right under the Copyright, Designs and Patents Act, 1988,
to be identified as Author of this work.
For legal purposes any Acknowledgements constitute
an extension of this copyright page.
Cover design by Boom Graduates Ltd and the Book Cover Zone USA.

All rights are reserved. No part of this publication may be reproduced or transmitted in any form or by any means, electronic or mechanical, including photocopying, recording, or any information storage or retrieval system, without prior permission in writing from the publishers.

Boom Publications Ltd do not have any control over, or responsibility for any third-party websites referred to or in this book. All internet addresses given in this book were correct at the time of going to press. The author and publisher regret any inconvenience if addresses have changed or sites have ceased to exist, but can accept no responsibility for any such changes.

Typeset by Helen at Boom Graduates.
Printed and bound in the UK.

To find out more about our authors and books visit www.boomgraduates.com
and sign up for our newsletters.

Ellen Harrold

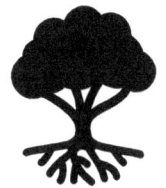

We plant a tree for every
Boom Graduate book commissioned, and
thereafter plant a tree for every 10 books sold.

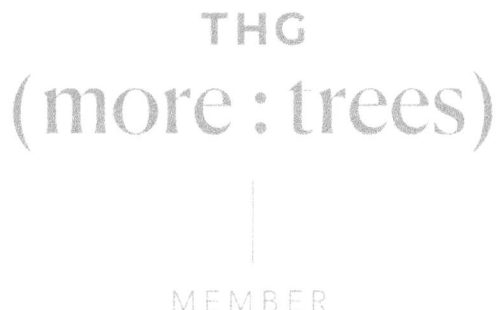

Watch our forest grow at
https://moretrees.eco/forest/BoomPublicationsLtd/

The Aesthetics and Conventions of Medical Art

Ellen Harrold

The Aesthetics and Conventions of Medical Art

The Aesthetics and Conventions of Medical Art

Ellen Harrold

Contents

Author biography..9
List of Figures 11
Introduction..15
Chapter One: Renaissance Medical Art...................................21
Chapter Two: 19th Century Medical Art..................................45
Chapter Three: Contemporary Medical Art............................73
Conclusion..99
References...107
Acknowledgements 113
Artist's images 115
BOOM! 125
A note about Boom Graduates...127
Notes 131

The Aesthetics and Conventions of Medical Art

Ellen Harrold

Author biography

Ellen Harrold is an artist focused on the human connection to science and nature. She is currently completing a Masters degree in Art, Science, and Visual thinking at Dundee University and has received a Bachelors degree in Fine Art from IADT in Dublin. A core aspect of her practice is the use of painting, drawing, text, and textiles to explore the connection between decay and renewal in the fundamental structure of the world around us. At the moment she is focused on how scientific understanding was, and continues to be understood through the lens of art and storytelling. She has taken part in IADT student shows such as New Translations in IMMA (2019), On Show in IADT (2022) and Propositions in IADT (2022).She has also recently published both written and visual work in New Feathers Anthology (Winter 2022), Londemere Literary (Issue 1), and Honeyguide Literary (Issue 5).

The Aesthetics and Conventions of Medical Art

Ellen Harrold

List of Figures

With special thanks to Christine Borland, and Ella Maru Studio, for their generous permission to use images of their work within this book.

Fig. 1, Andreas Vesalius, *Third Nerve Figure*, 1543, Woodcut print.

Fig. 2, Andreas Vesalius, *Male Figure Showing Veins and Arteries*, 1543, Woodcut print.

Fig. 3, Andreas Vesalius, *Female Torso Revealing Urinary system*, 1543, Woodcut print.

Fig. 4, Apollonios, *Belvedere Torso*, Unknown, Marble Statue.

Fig. 5, Leonardo Da Vinci, *Studies of Arm Muscles*, 1507-08, Ink on Paper.

Fig. 6, Andreas Vesalius, *Figure of Suspended Vein System*, 1543, Woodcut print.

Fig. 7, Andreas Vesalius, *Drawing of the brain*, 1543, Woodcut print.

Fig. 8, Nicholas-Henry Jacob, *The Axilla and Neck*, 1830, Lithographic print.

Fig. 9, Anon, *The Four Seasons- Autumnus*, 17th Century, Copperplate Engraving.

Fig. 10, Anon, *The Four Seasons- Autumnus*, 17th Century, Copperplate Engraving.

Fig. 11, Nicholas-Henry Jacob, *Facial Muscles*, 1830, Lithographic print.

Fig. 12, Nicholas-Henry Jacob, *Vein Network of the Head and Neck*, 1830, Lithographic print.

Fig. 13, Vesalius, *Partial DIssection of the Brain*, 1543, Woodblock print.

Fig. 14, Nicholas-Henry Jacob, *Heart valves and fibrous connective tissue of the heart*, 1830, Lithographic print.

Fig. 15, Guillaume-Benjamin-Amand Duchenne, *A Scene of Coquetry*, 1862, Photograph.

Fig. 16, Andreas Vesalius, *Ecorche*, 1543, Woodblock print.

Fig. 17, Jean-Baptiste Marc Bourgery, *Internal Organs*, 1854, Lithographic print.

Fig. 18, Christine Borland, *Cast From Nature*, 2011, Plaster.

Fig. 19, Chris Flask, the lungs of healthy volunteers (left) and cystic fibrosis (CF) patients (right), 2020, Quantitative T1 MRI mapping.

Fig. 20, AXIAL3D, *3D Printed Organs*, 2019, Plastic 3D printed sculpture.

Fig. 21, Christine Borland ,*Did I Request Thee, Maker, From my Clay to Mould Me Man? Did I Solicit Thee From Darkness to Promote Me?*, 1997, Ink on Paper.

Fig. 22, Christine Borland, *From Life*, 1994-1997, Mixed Media.

Fig. 23, Christine Borland, *From Life*, 1994-1997, Mixed Media.

Fig. 24, Christine Borland, *From Life*, 1994-1997, Mixed Media.

Fig. 25, Santiago Ramón y Cajal, *Glial cells of the cerebral cortex of a child*, 1904, Ink on Paper.

Fig. 26, Ella Maru Studio, *Bacterial hairs power nature's electric grid*, 2021, Digital Render.

Fig. 27, Christine Borland, *Bullet Proof Breath*, 2001, Glass and Spider Silk.

Fig. 28, Ellen Harrold, *Anatomical studies, 2022, Charcoal on Paper.*

Fig. 29, Ellen Harrold, *Anatomical studies, 2022, Charcoal on Paper.*

Fig. 30, Ellen Harrold, *Figure Rotation, 2022, Pencil on Paper.*

Fig. 31, Ellen Harrold, *Ligament Reconstruction, 2022, Acrylic, Wool, and Nettle on Canvas.*

Ellen Harrold

Introduction

Medical art has always been a discipline built on innovation and study, constantly changing to suit our understanding of the human body. Dominant religious, cultural and scientific belief have always played a key role in that understanding, even as we strive for impartiality. Every form of communication and visual depiction is built on the foundation of cultural understanding and the complex history of the people making it, especially aspects of communication that one can take for granted such as the direction that we read in and the use of literal depictions come down to a shared cultural understanding that shifts and evolves. To break down the entirety of cultural influence is impossible because every piece of art is ultimately a response to culture, even as we try to distance ourselves from that fact. Instead, I aimed to interrogate these influences from a historical perspective so that I could begin to examine the course and trajectory of contemporary medical art. Based on the current state of medical art practice which is currently in a period of rapid development and experimentation, I identified two periods which showed similar patterns in terms of artistic experimentation and development: the Renaissance and the Industrial Revolution.

I hope to discuss and analyse how the current theory and methodology of medical art has evolved from its predecessors. Was it a deliberate process of development and refinement like the study of the sciences or a process of experimentation and exploration more akin to the arts? All too often we treat medicine and science as fixed points, based purely on logic and facts beyond the influence of culture and popular opinion, when history shows us that that is never the case. Information is a cultural exchange, reliant on shared understandings. This is never more prevalent than when one discusses the human body, especially in a medical context. By examining the development of modern medical art from its inception in Renaissance Europe to the modern day, I aim to show how medical art is both a record of scientific inquiry and consensus and a reflection of our philosophical understanding of the human body and the physical self. To open this discussion and establish the historical and artistic evidence behind my assessment I will be asking "How did the aesthetics and conventions of contemporary medical art develop?" and analysing this information through the lens of a cultural and artistic exchange, rather than through the scientific accuracy, artistic merit, or efficacy of the works in question.

Over the course of this book I will be exploring two periods of major development in the history of medical art practice. Chapter one will centre on the mid to late Renaissance focusing on the work of Andreas Vesalius, particularly his treatise on anatomy 'De Humani Corporis Fabrica Libri Septem', which heralded the transition from galenic theory and practise in the study of medicine to a more modernised theory based on observation and visual interrogation. For chapter two I focus on the work of Jean Baptiste-Marc Bourgery, including his anatomical atlas 'Traité complet de l'anatomie de l'homme', which was published in 1866–1871 through the midst of the industrial revolution, culminating the traditional of realism in medical art and beginning the process of stylisation that dominates contemporary medical art. Both of these periods were characterised by swift and dramatic scientific and technological development, resulting in widespread cultural changes and an explosion of experimental art practices. This also allows the historical context to reflect the analysis of contemporary medical art practice that will be examined in chapter three. For this chapter I examine the work of Christine Borland, whose sculptural and digital work has bridged the gap between medical art and the gallery space. Resulting in a dialogue that has questioned the place of medical art in the annals of both history and art.

Contextualising medical art is essential in acknowledging it as an artistic and communicative process. Treating it as a simple, objective representation of fact can be comforting as it takes human error, and miscommunication can be comforting as it means that what we see and know about our bodies has reached its final conclusion - there are no biases to confront and no inaccuracies to obstruct our understanding. Yet, it will evolve, perhaps in ways that are unimaginable to us now, but it will surely continue to develop and reflect our understanding of the physical self.

The Aesthetics and Conventions of Medical Art

Ellen Harrold

Chapter One

Renaissance Medical Art

The foundations of contemporary medical art are primarily Euro-centric due to colonialist efforts to suppress the continued development of information and research that challenged or subverted predominant European practices. The emerging homogeneity of emerging medical theories and art over hundreds of years due to colonial expansion and control has contributed heavily to medical art's linear development, which began to take on its current shape during the Renaissance.[1] Before this point, medical practice was predominantly guided by the teachings of ancient Greek and

---

[1] Lesley A. Sharp, "The Commodification of the Body and its Parts", Annual Review of Anthropology (Vol 29, 2000) p. 306.

Roman sources such as Pliny the Elder and Galen, whose instruction was spread through the use of manuscripts.[2] While there are numerous examples of anatomical and medical drawings and prints, these were more commonly used as instructional guides to field surgery and wound care, rather than the anatomical recordings and scientific diagrams that we associate with medical art today. The lack of anatomy based medical art can be attributed to the costly nature of reproducing such works to a wide audience, as well as the prevailing beliefs of Galen, who believed that illustrations were a poor substitute for first hand studies of the human body.[3] While many believe that the lack of anatomical art is due to the influence of the Catholic church and taboos around dissection, there is ample evidence that

---

[2] Faye Getz, *Medicine in the English Middle Ages* (Princeton University Press, 1998) p.36.
[3] Isabelle Pantin, "Analogy and Difference: A Comparative Study of Medical and Astronomical Images in Books" in Nicholas Jardine and Isla Fay's (Ed.) <u>Observing the World Through Images: Diagrams and Figures in the Early-Modern Arts and `Sciences</u>. (Leiden, Brill. 2014), p.15.

the stagnation of medical art continued long after dissection became widely accepted and practiced.[4]

The Renaissance launched medical art into a period of rapid development and innovation, with large scale print blocks making medical texts more cost efficient and widely available and allowing them to prove their worth as learning aids and visual guides to the human body. Many physicians and anatomists began using anatomical drawings as support for their discoveries and theories, which allowed the art to take on an exploratory and discursive framework that separated it from strictly representational anatomy art.[5] One of the most renowned pioneers of medical art during this time period was arguably Andreas Vesalius, who lived from 1514 to 1564 and is heralded as the father of modern anatomy. His treatise on anatomy 'De humani corporis

---

[4] Katherine Park, "The Criminal and the Saintly Body: Autopsy and Dissection in Renaissance Italy" Renaissance Quarterly (Vol 47, No 1, Spring 1994) p. 3.

[5] Domenico Laurenza, "Art and Anatomy: Images from a Scientific Revolution" The Metropolitan Mueseum of Art bulletin. (Vol 69, No 3, Winter 2012) p. 8.

fabrica libri septem' is the foundation of modern medical practice, adopting an observation-based approach to the human body based on interrogation and proof.[6] This is not to say that he denied or refuted classical approaches to medicine, in fact he believed the issue to be that physicians were misinterpreting or poorly applying these approaches.[7] While Vesalius's scientific theories may not necessarily be relevant to the art that he produced, his respect and admiration for classical schools of thought are a cornerstone in the artistic representation of the human form in Fabrica.

Greco-Roman influences are apparent throughout the illustrations of Vesalius's work, most notably in the posing and illustrative qualities seen in his depiction of the human figure. The use of contrapposto, the emphasis on physical idealism, and the way that the torso is often sectioned off from the rest of the figure are the most predominant

---

[6] Gillian Furlong, *Treasures from UCL* (UCL Press, 2015) p. 24.
[7] Roberto Lo Presti, "Anatomy as Epistemology: The Body of Man and the Body of Medicine in Vesalius and his Ancient Sources (Celsus, Galen)" Renaissance and Reformation (Vol 33, No 3, Summer 2010) pp. 31-32.

examples of the Greco-Roman influences that had long guided medical theory. Of course, these artistic flourishes were also incredibly popular during the Renaissance and a defining aspect of art during this era. What begs further investigation is the relationship between these historic motifs and the exploratory nature of Vesalius's work, which relied on accuracy and clinical observation.

One of the most obvious examples of the influences of Greco-Roman antiquity in Vesalius's depiction of the human body is in the posing of the models throughout his Fabrica. These models are not depicted as dissected bodies on a dissection table but as standing figures, often depicted against the background of port towns or sprawling countryside. The posing of the figures is also reminiscent of classical sculpture, with the iconic use of contrapposto and emphasis on naturalistic movement at the focal point of the composition and design.[8] It is important to say that when I say his figurative work, I am describing how Vesalius

---

[8] David Summers, "Contrapposto: Style and Meaning in Renaissance Art" The Art Bulletin (Vol 59, No 3, September 1997) pp. 360-361.

depicted the entirety of the human form, regardless of whether or not it is interconnected by skeletal, muscular, or vascular structures. While these figures are consistently depicted using classical motifs, they are noticeably absent from Vesalius's schematic depictions of individual anatomical systems, as can be seen in Fig. 1 *Third Nerve Figure* where Vesalius has depicted the nervous system of the torso and left arm in a simple pose facing the viewer. This could be attributed to the popularity of humanism at the time, or a homage to the importance that Vesalius placed on holistic medical practices and the unity of the medical profession.[9] It should be noted that Vesalius's diagrams of individual pieces of human anatomy, such as the brain and heart, are consistently rendered in a much more realistic style. The anatomical objects are consistently depicted from a top-down perspective as one would see them on an operating table, with the body depicted as a rigid cadaver. This divide between the explorative diagrams and established figurative

---

[9] Lo Presti, p. 31.

work reflects the beginning of the break away from traditional practice and the work that Vesalius would pioneer as he began the shift away from the teachings of classical medical practitioners such as Galen.[10]

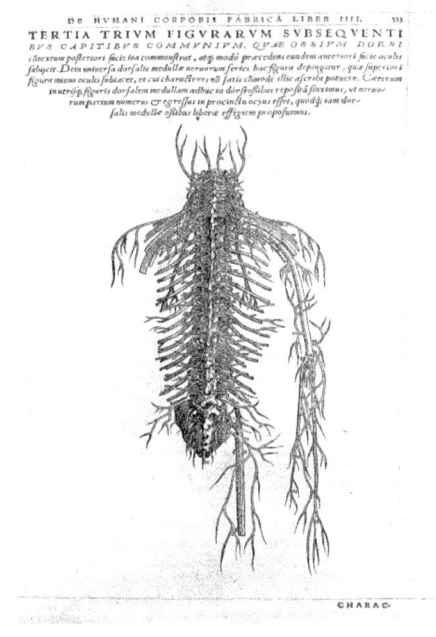

Fig. 1, Andreas Vesalius, *Third Nerve Figure*, Woodcut print, 1543.

---

[10] Laurenza, pp. 22-23.

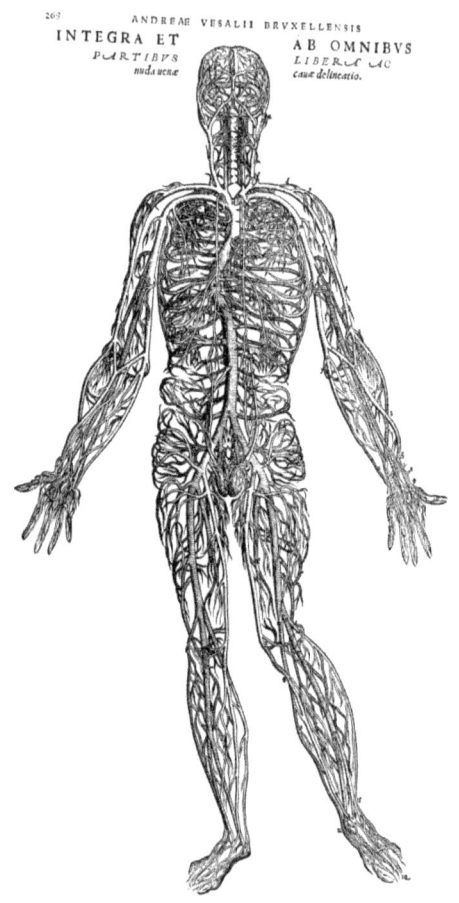

Fig. 2, Andreas Vesalius,
Male Figure Showing Veins and Arteries, Woodcut print, 1543.

Ellen Harrold

The physical resemblance to Greco-Roman sculpture can also be seen in the prints that focus on the torso and its internal organs, with the sectioning of the body cutting off the head and limbs in a style reminiscent of many sculptural artefacts.[11] *The Belvedere Torso*, seen in fig. 4, was unearthed in the lead up to Fabrica's production, follows a similar sectioning of the body, with the legs cut off mid-thigh, the arms cut off just below the shoulder, and the neck cut off just above where it meets the shoulders.[12] While the placement of these cut-off points could be attributed to coincidence, the uneven cut-off points and asymmetrical nature of the sectioning is much more illustrative of the artistic influence of classical statues.[13]

---

[11] Leonard Barkan, "The Beholder's Tale: Ancient Sculpture, Renaissance Narratives" Representations (No 44, Autumn 1993) p. 134.
[12] Glenn Harcourt, "Andreas Vesalius and the Anatomy of Antique Sculpture" Representations (No 17, Special Issue: The Cultural Display of the Body, Winter 1987) pp. 30-31.
[13] Rachel Kousser, "Destruction and Memory on the Athenian Acropolis" The Art Bulletin (Vol 91, No 3, September 2009) p. 266.

The Aesthetics and Conventions of Medical Art

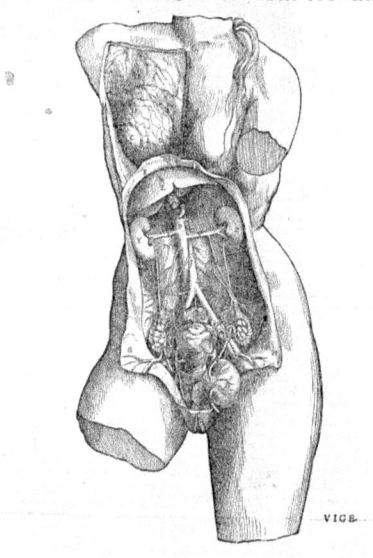

Fig. 3, Andreas Vesalius,
Female Torso Revealing Urinary system, Woodcut print, 1543.

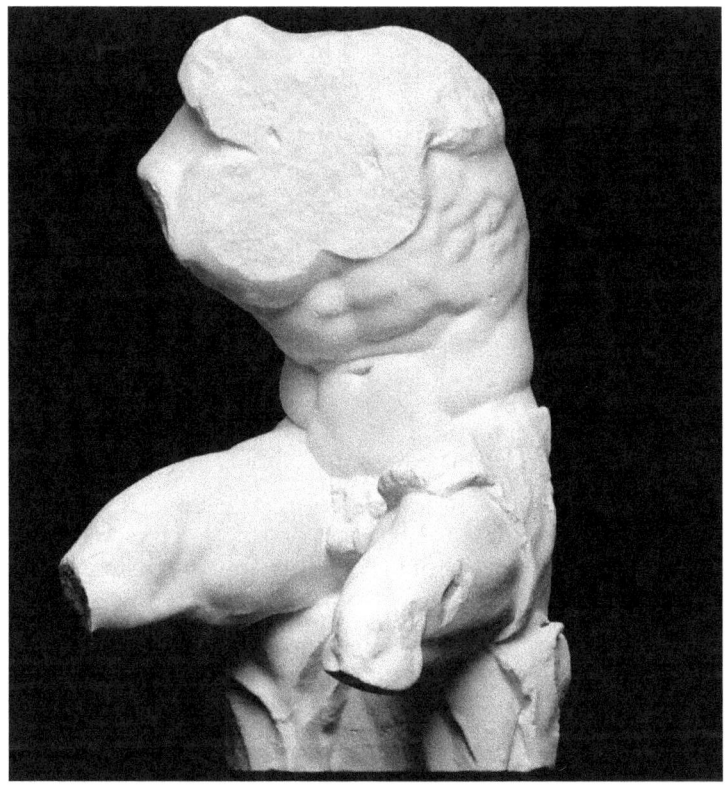

Fig. 4, Apollonios, *Belvedere Torso*, Marble Statue, Unknown.

The consistent depiction of idealised physiques and emphasis on musculature for the male body is a particularly striking remnant of classical artistic influences in Vesalius's

Fabrica. Given the limited availability and high turnover rate of cadavers[14] it is unlikely that many of Vesalius's subjects would have been in such good physical shape. Therefore, it can be assumed that the prevalence of such figures in his work must have been a result of artistic interpretation or careful selection of the bodies that were used for his illustrations. The depiction of these figures may have also been influenced by Titian, whose workshop is often credited with producing the plates for the fabrica.[15] Whether or not Titian's workshop was responsible for the prints, it is largely agreed that Vesalius did the preparatory sketches and directed their creation, thus one can safely say that the aesthetic qualities were an intended aspect of the finished piece. The incorporation of aesthetic idealism is a key factor in the composition and design of these images, given the long-standing cultural association between health and

---

[14] Catrien Santing, "Andreas Vesalius's "De Fabrica corporis humana", depiction of the human model in word and image" Netherlands Yearbook for History of Art (Vol 58, 2007-2008) p. 59
[15] Harcourt, pp. 31-32.

beauty and the popularity of dissection theatres among the wealthy elite who would be among the limited audience for published books.[16]

Anatomy studies and art as a method of anatomical investigation were at their height during the Renaissance, with artists such as Leonardo da Vinci and Antonio Pollaiuolo conducting many thorough and well documented investigations in the function of human form.[17] Da Vinci's journals have been particularly renowned for their anatomical accuracy and their investigative qualities, which focused on not only surface level observational anatomy, but the mathematical and biological breakdown of the human form. Where Da Vinci's doctrine of investigation differed from Vesalius's was in the practical application of knowledge and the line of questioning involved, Drawing by Da Vinci such as *Drawing of Vitruvian Man* as seen in Fig. 4

---

[16] Santing, pp. 59-67.

[17] Charles Singer, "Notes on Renaissance Artists and Practical Anatomy" Journal of the History of Medicine and Allied Sciences (Vol 5, No 2, Spring 1950) pp. 156-158.

demonstrates a questioning of why the human form exists in its corporeal state, whereas Vesalius was primarily focused on how it exists as an interactive series of mechanisms. The technique that Vesalius pioneered was not the co-operative use of art and science, rather it was the use of art as a support structure for science rather than science as a support structure for art. While his process was initially met with scepticism from those who continued to follow Galenic tradition, the meticulous quality of his research and the detailed accuracy of the art that illustrated it set the foundations of medical art as we know it today. Vesalius's innovative practice of merging detailed practical descriptions, observational research with schematic, finely formulated diagrams was revolutionary. The result of this approach was a text that offered extensive support in the observation of dissections, giving medical practitioners a stable reference upon which they could base their practical skills.

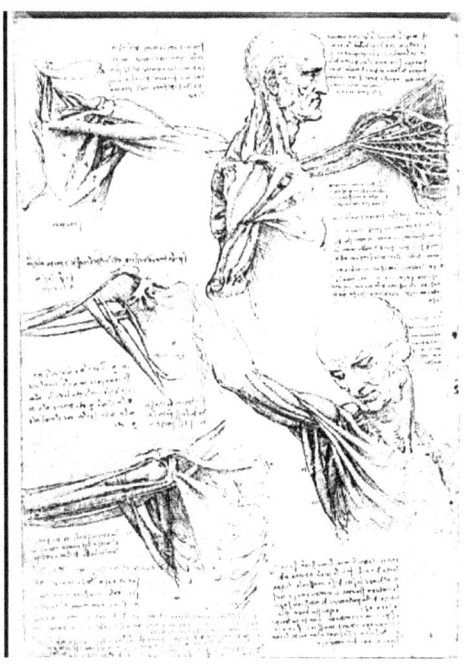

Fig. 5, Leonardo Da Vinci, *Studies of Arm Muscles*, Ink on Paper, 1507-08.

Vesalius changed the course of European medical art by proving that images could supplement and support the tried and tested practices of dissection and observation rather than existing as an inferior form of education. He achieved this by adopting a myriad of innovative approaches such as depicting the body as both an entire system and as individual parts, his use of top-down perspective, and the incredible detail of his prints. The depiction of the body as a complete structure and a series of individual parts is particularly notable due to the fact that it was a widespread practice amongst artists, at the time, but rarely seen in medical manuscripts. Leonardo da Vinci's notebooks come to mind, in particular, with his studies of muscular and skeletal systems and his breakdown of their individual mechanics.[18] While this approach was well known among artists, this approach to depicting anatomical systems was rarely used in medical art as the illustration that existed in the traditional guides to wound care and illness primarily focused on treatment rather than anatomical structure.[19] By bringing these artistic techniques to the medical art canon Vesalius introduced the diagrammatic technique of separating

---

[18] Jonathan Pevsner, "Leonardo da Vinci, Neuroscientist" Scientific American Mind (Vol 16, No 1, 2005) pp. 84-86.

[19] Faye Getz, *Medicine in the English Middle Ages* (Princeton, Princeton University Press, 1998) p. 40.

information to the medical art canon.[20] This meant that medical art would use multiple diagrams to display several aspects of information which could then be examined as a whole, rather than the traditional approach of including as much information in a single diagram as possible. This approach improved the quality and legibility of the information being presented, as well as, allowing each diagram to become more visually detailed and intricate. The same approach can be seen in Da Vinci's work, particularly in the vast array of movements seen in his *Studies of Arm Muscles*.

---

[20] Isabelle Pantin, "Analogy and Difference: A Comparative Study of Medical and Astronomical Images in Books" in Nicholas Jardine and Isla Fay's (Ed.) Observing the World Through Images: Diagrams and Figures in the Early-Modern Arts and `Sciences. (Leiden, Brill. 2014), pp. 40-43

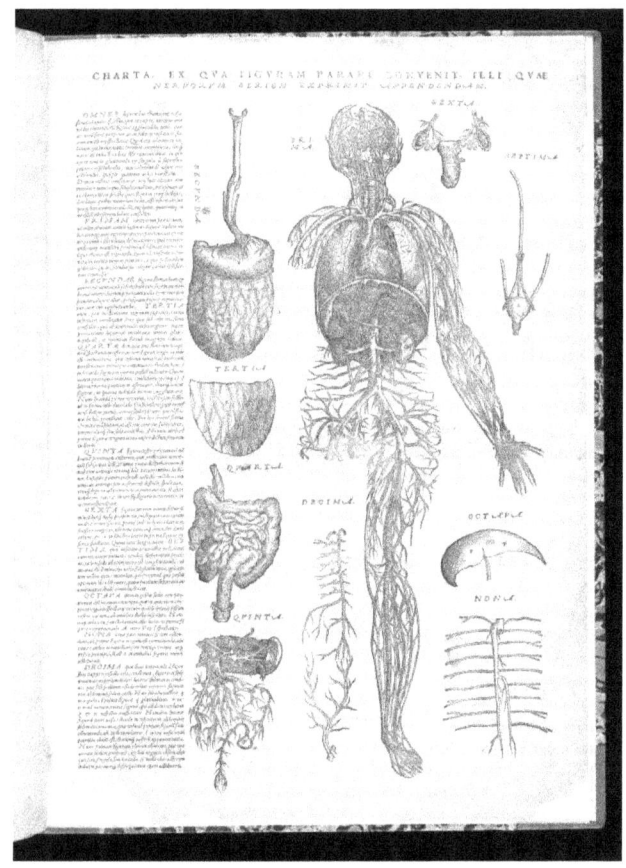

Fig. 6, Andreas Vesalius,
Figure of Suspended Vein System, Woodcut print, 1543.

Vesalius's approach to analysing and depicting individual anatomical parts differs from his approach to the whole human form, with the figures being depicted as living people and the anatomical pieces in situ as dissected cadavers.[21] This is possibly due to the influences of Humanism and the cultural importance of the human figure having superiority over an 'object' as defined by prevailing Christian beliefs at the time. The lack of artistic importance and pressure to uphold traditional aesthetic traditions allowed Vesalius to explore a more practical style of anatomical art, wherein the subjects are depicted with a top-down perspective as one would observe them on an anatomy table. This made Fabrica much more effective as a reference tool and more importantly, it streamlined and standardised Fabrica's prints. This step towards a systematic approach to representations established a mode of practice for other publications to follow.[22] Paving the way for Vesalius's template for medical

---

[21] Martin Kemp, *Picturing Knowledge: Historical and Philosophical Problems Concerning the Use of Art in Science* (Toronto, University of Toronto Press, 1996) p. 56.

[22] Zlatko I. Pozeg, Eugene S. Flamm, "Vesalius and the 1543 Epitome of his "De humani corporis Fabrica librorum": A Uniquely Illuminated Copy" The Papers of the Bibliographical Society of America (Vol 103, No 2, 2009. p.200.

art allowed the practice to proliferate amongst medical texts, with some practitioners even using Vesalius's diagrams to illustrate their own works for years to come.[23]

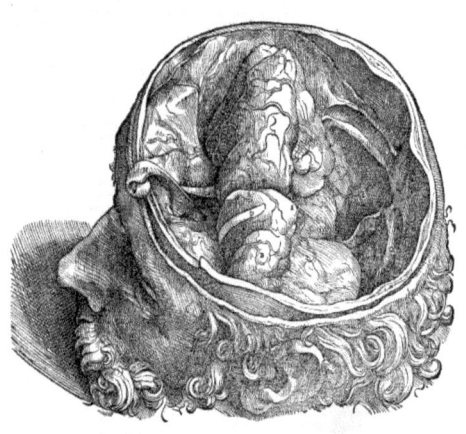

Fig. 7, Andreas Vesalius, *Drawing of the brain*, Woodcut print, 1543.

---

[23] David L Martin, *Curious Visions of Modernity : Enchantment, Magic, and the Sacred*, (London, The MIT Press, 2011) p. 67.

The exploratory approach to artistic anatomy study popular amongst artists at the time also seems to have been particularly influential in Vesalius's aesthetic approach to medical art. Many of his diagrams are reminiscent of observational sketches rather than the illustrative, stylised diagrams that were previously associated with medical art.[24] This can be attributed to technological advances at the time, which made prints cheaper to produce and allowed them to have much more detail and accuracy.[25] The exceptional quality and aesthetic appeal of the prints allowed the manuscript to serve as a reference guide for observing a dissection which was well received by the growing scores of academics and nobles who flocked to the ever-increasing numbers of dissection theatres. This ever-growing market of wealthy medical enthusiasts appreciated the book's aesthetic

---

[24]Harry Clark, "Foiling the Pirates: The Preparation and Publication of Andreas Vesalius's De Humani Corporis Fabrica" The Library Quarterly: Information, Community, Policy (Vol 51, No 3, 1981) p. 302.

[25] Peter Parshall, "Introduction: The Modern Historiography of Early Printmaking" Studies in the History of Art (Vol 75, 2009) pp. 9-10.

appeal and intricate detail over the practicality and plainness of other illustrated medical manuscripts.[26] This also created a demand for medical texts among collectors, creating a market that medical artists enthusiastically catered to.[27] This widespread popularity granted the genre of art much needed legitimacy and soon it proliferated through universities and began to garner academic favour granting the art form both legitimacy and demand.

This period of development in medical art marked the first step toward the modernisation of medical practice and the beginnings of the visual culture of medicine as we know it today. Even as the influences of cultural context and the barriers of history separates Vesalius's work from our contemporary understanding of medical art practice it remains recognizable as a forerunner to modern medical art

---

[26] Paula Findlen, "Possessing the Past: The Material World of the Italian Renaissance" The American Historical Review (Vol 103, No 1, February 1998) pp. 86-87.

[27] Harry Clark, "Foiling the Pirates: The Preparation and Publication of Andreas Vesalius's De Humani Corporis Fabrica" The Library Quarterly: Information, Community, Policy (Vol 51, No 3, 1981) pp. 303- 306.

practice. His merging of strict observational analysis combined with the use of stylised, iconic imagery and precise use of linework made these images effective learning and reference tools that retained an aesthetic quality that made them ripe for collectors. Ensuring their longevity as art pieces and their dissipation amongst the wider populace. While many factors played into the proliferation of Vesalius's work such as the availability of books due to the printing press and the illustrative capabilities of woodblock prints.

Vesalius's work legitimised the use of medical art in Europe, granting practitioners the credence they needed to explore and innovate the practice. With the consistent improvements in printing technology and the increasing availability of books, medical art began to play a key role in the education of medical practitioners. These texts not only improved the standards of medical education, they also served as a way to spread new ideas and innovations in the science of anatomy and medicine. The wide availability of these books and their illustrations also equalised the standards of care across Europe and allowed more people to contribute to the advancement of medical science. Expanding the practice of medical art and allowing it to flourish and develop throughout the world. These works also serve as a record of our understanding of the human body, health, and surgery through the ages. Documenting the merge and separation of culture, religion, and science through our understanding of the physical self, it's not until the 19th century that we begin to see another period of such rapid evolution in the practice of medical art. This time characterised by the technological advancement, proliferation of information, and social pressures of the Industrial Revolution.

Ellen Harrold

Chapter Two

19th Century Medical Art

The expansion and rapid development of medical art in the Renaissance brought the practice into a period of steady incline over the next two centuries. As prints became more refined and cheaper to produce, medical art became a staple in universities and academic circles, granting the art form legitimacy and inspiring many academics and artists to document and publish their own findings. The next 400 years brought steady advancements in the communicative technique and scientific accuracy of medical art, with developments such as the use of wax figures and the ever increasing emphasis on realism, which expanded the scope and accuracy of the art.[28] As a result medical art became more and more comprehensive, proliferating amongst academics and collectors while also cementing itself as a vital framework for anatomical understanding and medical discourse.[29] It was not until the 19th century that we began to see another period of change in the use of medical art's technological advances, and emerging medical discourse continued to change the way that practitioners understood and depicted the human body.

The 19th century was a time of great innovation as the industrial revolution brought technology to the forefront of an already rapidly changing society. As a result of these technological advances medical equipment became more sophisticated and medical research became easier to conduct

---

[28] Martin Kemp and Marina Wallace, <u>Spectacular Bodies: The Art and Science of the Human Body from Leonardo to Now.</u> (London, Hayward Gallery and University of California Press, 2000) pp. 46-59.

[29] Londa Schiebinger, "Skeletons in the Closet: The First Illustrations of the Female Skeleton in Eighteenth-Century Anatomy", <u>Representations</u> (No. 14, Spring 1986) pp. 49-54.

and cheaper to publish.[30] These advances in medical science required an ever increasing amount of literature to illustrate and spread their ideas among practitioners throughout the world, with many traditional sources now proven to be clinically inaccurate a wave of new literature was created to take their place.[31] Two inventions crucial to this wave of medical literature were the photograph and the lithographic print which eliminated many of the boundaries of representation that had limited medical arts accuracy and scope.[32] Dealing with the difficult task of reconciling new discoveries with verifiable facts and a desperate race to present the most up to date clinical information to the masses, medical artists began to treat aesthetics as a tool for communication rather than a divine vocation. This shift

---

[30] Michael Worboys, "Practice and the Science of Medicine in the Nineteenth Century", Isis (Vol. 102, No. 1, March 2011) pp. 111-115.

[31] Michael Sappol, "Mr Joseph Maclise and the Epistemology of the Anatomical closet" British Art Studies (Issue 20, July 2021) See: https://doi.org/10.17658/issn.2058-5462/issue-20/msappol. Accessed 20 October 2021.

[32] Chris Amirault, "Posing the Subject of Early Medical Photography", Discourse (Vol. 16, No. 2, Winter 1993-94) pp. 51-57.

pulled the dominant style of medical art away from the iconographic style, classical motifs, and Christian themes of Renaissance medical art into a more realistic, detailed, diagrammatic style.

One of the most influential and widely distributed medical texts of this era was Jean-Baptiste Marc Bourgery's anatomical atlas, the Traité complet de l'anatomie de l 'homme which was published from 1831-1854.[33] Bourgery's eight volume treatise on anatomy was a comprehensive overview of existing anatomical knowledge alongside Bourgery's own research, embellished with 726 anatomical lithographic prints.[34] These prints were created by the artist Nicholas-Henry Jacob, and displayed a vast array of anatomical structures, as well as surgical techniques in incredibly fine detail, and with later editions printed in full colour. Along with the influence of the neoclassical artist Jacque-Louis David, whom Jacob had trained under, one

---

[33] David Macaulay, "Review: The Body Sketchers ", The Wilson Quarterly (Vol. 30, No. 4, Autumn 2006), pp. 109-110.
[34] Cindy Stelmackowich, "The art of Anatomical Science" Canadian Medical Association Journal. (Vol. 175, No. 5, 2006) p. 506.

can also see a shift from realism to stylisation in the depiction of individual anatomical parts and the human form.[35] Bourgery's atlas is also an excellent example of the techniques that were developed to demonstrate and understand physiological processes, especially in the areas of microscopic anatomy, embryonic development, and the nervous system.[36]

At this point in history medical texts were primarily being used by practitioners and students as an aid to the observation of dissection in surgical theatres. This is heavily attributed to the exorbitant cost of newly published texts, which were almost exclusively bought by universities and wealthy collectors.[37] While publishing was becoming cheaper and more advanced, medical texts were not following the same pattern, instead they remained an

---

[35] Tina Craig, "Treasures of the Library No 15", Royal College of Surgeons Bulletin (Vol. 81, No. 5, 1999)

[36] Julie V. Hansen and Suzanne Porter, The Physician's Art: Representations of Art and Medicine. (Durham, Duke University Library and Duke University Museum of Art, 1999), p. 61.

[37] Craig.

expensive commodity but the quality of the texts increased using more illustrations as well as becoming longer and more detailed. One of the most important developments in publicising was the emergence of lithographic printing. Lithographic printing is a chemical process that increases or decreases areas of absorption on a porous stone, allowing ink to be absorbed in different shades and textures. This printing technique produces a much finer and more detailed image than the traditional woodblock or copper plate print produces fewer disturbances on the paper due to being a planographic process.[38] However, arguably the most beneficial aspect of lithographic printing to medical artists is the ability to produce a wide variety of graphic effects and textures that are often limited by other forms of printing. This gave artists like Nicholas-Henry Jacob the ability to reproduce the textural differences between skin, muscle and nervous tissue with a lifelike accuracy that gave these

---

[38] Emil Ganso, H. W. Janson, "The Technique of Lithographic Printing", Parnassus (Vol. 12, No. 7, November 1940), pp. 16-19.

detailed prints their legibility and dimensionality.[39] While complex prints were previously limited to line work in order to retain their legibility, contrasting textures meant that complex, detailed diagrams could retain readability. This was instrumental in the production of Bourgery's anatomical atlas as he often chose to depict multiple detailed anatomical aspects, such as bone, muscle and internal organs in a single drawing. Texture was key in separating and defining each anatomical part while depicting them as a unified object, allowing a more accurate depiction of the human body as a whole. This use of texture quickly became a key aspect of medical representation, to the point where even the most simplified modern medical diagrams will use it as a key form of recognition and identification.[40]

---

[39] Macaulay, p. 110.
[40] Brian Williams and Linda Cameron, "Images in health care: potential and problems", Journal of Health Services Research & Policy, (Vol. 14, No. 4, October 2009) pp. 251-252.

The Aesthetics and Conventions of Medical Art

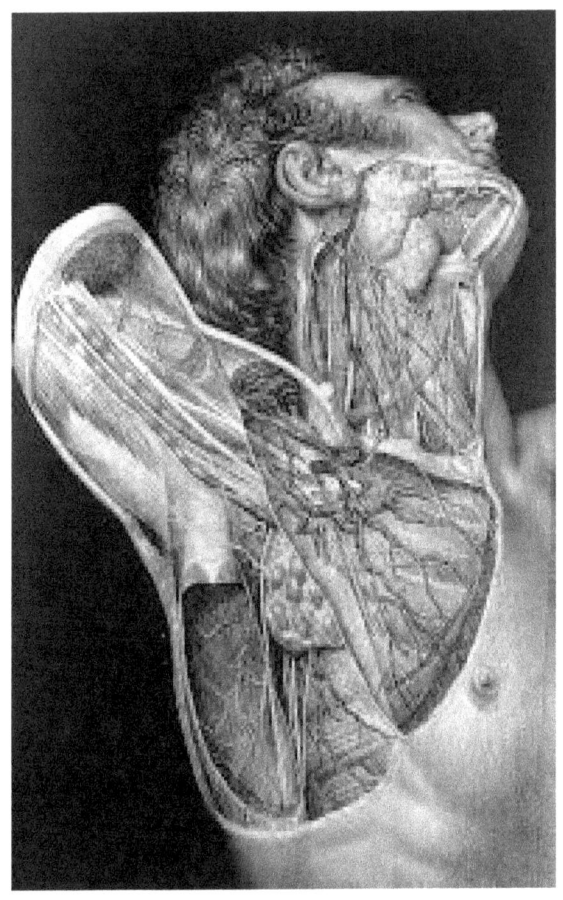

Fig. 8, Nicholas-Henry Jacob,
The Axilla and Neck, Lithographic print, 1830.

Bourgery's choice to utilise the depiction of combined anatomical aspects was also an excellent example of the developments in the utilisation of multi-level anatomical fugitive sheets. Anatomical fugitive sheets are illustrations made to display multiple levels of anatomy in a single drawing.[41] From the 15th century onwards this has been achieved through the use of hinged paper flaps which could be drawn back to display levels of anatomical artworks. While this was an innovative way to depict the interconnected nature of the body it was also inefficient in terms of reproduction, longevity and visual communication. What proved much more effective was the use of a stylised illustration that combined different aspects of anatomical layers into a single asymmetrical art piece. This technique may have been popularised and refined during the 19th century; it was used in much earlier anatomical prints. One

---

[41] L. H. Wells, "The "Sabio" and "Sylvester" Families of Anatomical Fugitive Sheets: Note on a Pair of Sheets in the National Library of Medicine", Bulletin of the History of Medicine, (Vol. 40, No. 5, September 1966) pp. 468-469.

early example of this style can be seen in *"The Four Seasons-Autumnus"*, Fig. 8, which depicts a nude male and female figure standing side by side, each with one leg raised. The male figure is depicted with prominent veins in his left foot and left arm, while the right calf is shown as a silhouette with simplified stylised veins without any other alterations being made to any other parts of the figures.[42] While it is speculated that this may be a reference to bloodletting calendars, or possibly a reference to the story of Achilles, there is no solid indication in the work itself. [43] This style is distinct from Vesalius's depiction of partially dissected cadavers in that it is an active choice to depict two select internal anatomical structures from separate perspectives, rather than an observational drawing.[44]

---

[42] Hansen and Porter, pp.48-52.
[43] Jonathan, S. Burgess, The Death and Afterlife of Achilles. (Baltimore, Johns Hopkins University Press, 2009) pp. 9-13.
[44] Cindy Stelmackowich, "Bodies of Knowledge: The Nineteenth-Century Anatomical Atlas in the Spaces of Art and Science" Canadian Art Review. (Vol. 33 No. 1/2, 2008) p. 83.

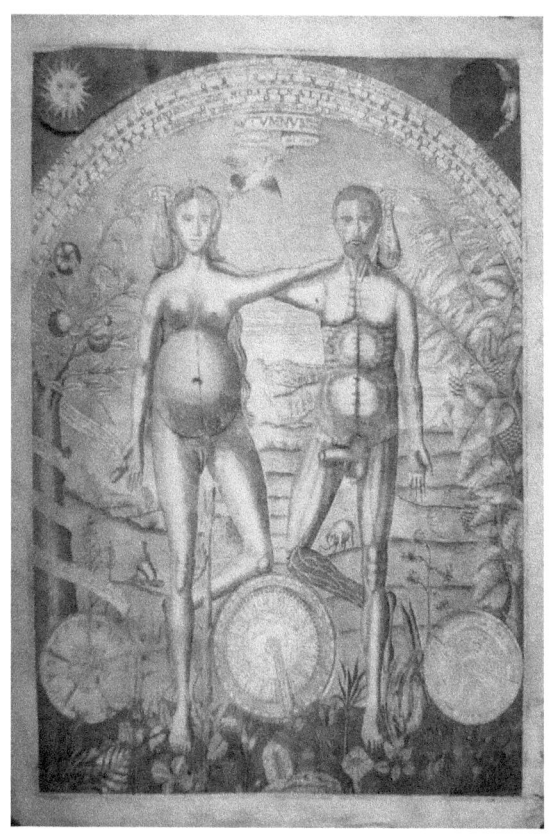

Fig. 9, Anon, *The Four Seasons- Autumnus*, Copperplate Engraving, 17th Century.

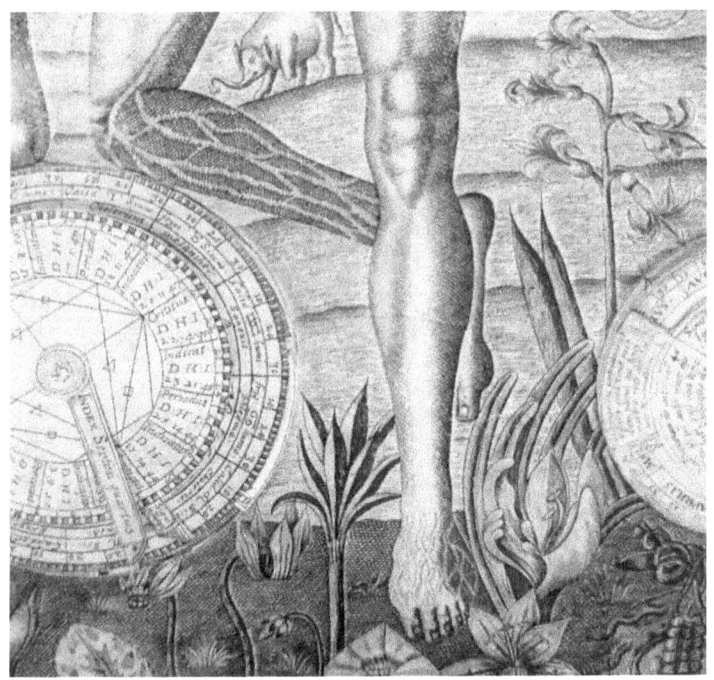

Fig. 10, Anon, *The Four Seasons- Autumnus*, Copperplate Engraving, 17th Century.

Bourgery's atlas expands on the communicative aspect of this style, using it to communicate the layering and connections of various tissues and organs in the body.[45] The

---

[45] Stelmackowich, p. 79.

development of this style of representation also reflected the more holistic approach to health and medicine that was gaining traction during this period, as people began to understand the causes and widespread impacts of disease and illness. Galenic theories based on the four humours and disease as a spiritual or cosmological event had lost their credibility as anatomists began to understand the role that cleanliness and the environment played in one's health.[46] This style of diagram not only enhanced the communicative qualities of the diagrams, it reflected the burgeoning understanding of our immune system and the body as an interconnected, responsive system. [47]

---

[46] Glen M. Cooper, "Numbers, Prognosis, and Healing: Galen on Medical Theory", Journal of the Washington Academy of Sciences. (Vol. 90, No.2, Summer 2004) pp. 45-48.

[47] Stelmackowich, pp. 76-77.

The Aesthetics and Conventions of Medical Art

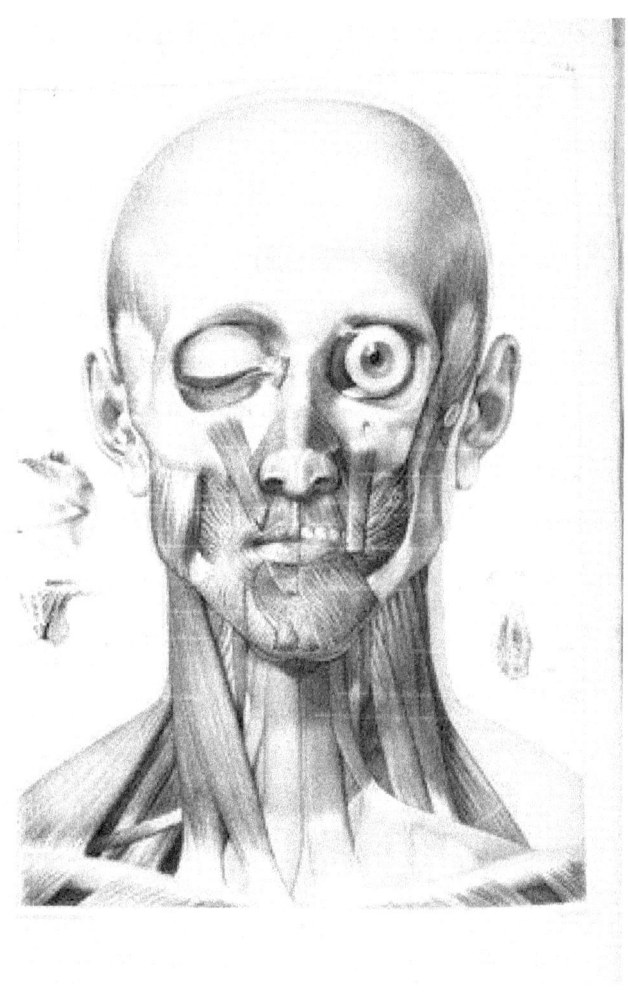

Fig. 11, Nicholas-Henry Jacob, *Facial Muscles*, Lithographic print, 1830.

Bourgery's use of stylisation as a communication tool is also representative of the conflict between realism and stylisation that was occurring in medical art during this period as it became clear that clinical accuracy and artistic accuracy were two very different goals. Medical art may have retained the incredible level of detail and emphasis on observation but more and more interpretation was being required to represent medical fact in a visual format.[48] Simply drawing a sequence of the dissection process as accurately as possible did not lend itself to providing context to the process and often made it impossible to present the totality of an anatomical structure.[49] Most importantly, the observation-based approach to anatomical drawing was inefficient at communicating anatomical theory, as biological processes and anatomical structure rarely present themselves in a visible format. Visual communication required subtle changes, such as omitting the skin flaps around the area of

---

[48] Stelmackowich, p. 78.
[49] Stelmackowich, p. 79.

dissection, having different areas of the body depicted in different stages of movement, and showing the veins and nervous system intact over the areas that could not be accessed without damaging them.[50] One example of this can be seen when comparing Bourgery's depiction of the subcutaneous anatomy of the human head to Vesalius's dissection of the human brain, as seen in Fig. 11 and Fig. 12. Bourgery depicts the side profile of the figure on a blank surface with no shadows or background information, the face is expressionless and lacks any discernible facial features barring the bone structure of the face. Vesalius's work shows not only the shadows being cast on the table by the head, it also depicts the layers of skin that have been unevenly cut away as well as the distinctive facial features and hair of the figure in question. This shift can be accredited to the increasing importance of microscopic and movement based anatomical depictions, as well as the incredible popularity of anatomical wax models and the

---

[50] Hansen and Porter, p. 61.

introduction of the photograph.[51] Realism in print could no longer hold up against competing art forms, or meet the technical requirements needed to represent the bulk of medical theory that was swiftly coming to light.

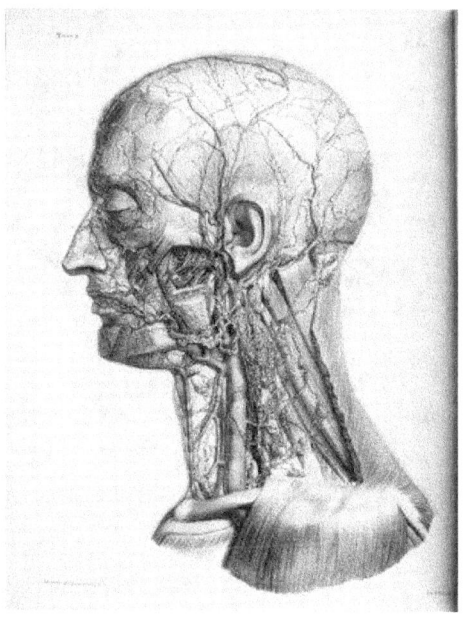

Fig. 12, Nicholas-Henry Jacob,
Vein Network of the Head and Neck, Lithographic print, 1830.

---

[51] Kemp and Wallace, p. 59

The Aesthetics and Conventions of Medical Art

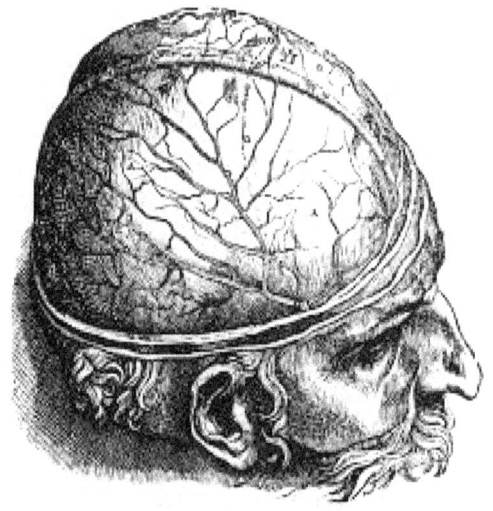

Fig. 13, Vesalius, *Partial DIssection of the Brain*,
Woodblock print, 1543.

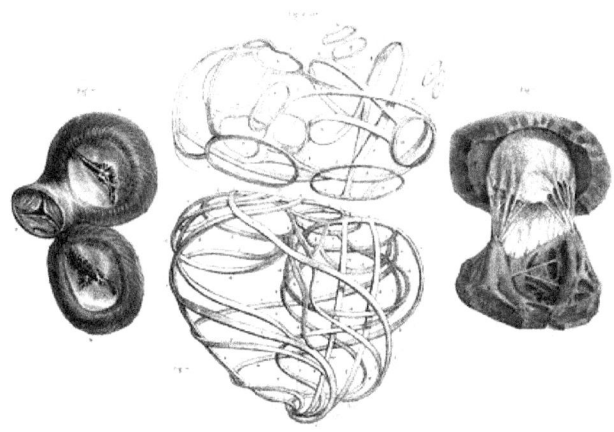

Fig. 14, Nicholas-Henry Jacob, *Heart valves and fibrous connective tissue of the heart*, Lithographic print, 1830.

The discovery of photography was a revolutionary step in the development of science and art, allowing one to record things at a speed and accuracy that is impossible to match.[52] Early photographers were quick to utilise this for the medical profession, extensively documenting physical

---

[52] Stelmackowich, pp. 81-82.

ailments amongst the living and the dead.[53] The use of photography as a record of samples and research made it particularly popular amongst physicians who needed to record a variety of symptoms or gather evidence quickly and methodically.[54] One such proponent was Guillaume-Benjamin-Amand Duchenne, a neurologist who used photography to examine changes in facial expression in reaction to emotional and physical stimuli, such as the electricity he used on a young woman in the photograph '*A Scene of Coquetry'* as seen in Fig. 14.[55] A feat that would have been unreliable and enormously time consuming if attempted with the use of traditional art practices. While this fierce competition certainly pushed the use of stylisation amongst medical artists in order to compete, the first photograph was taken in 1826, only four years before Bourgery's Traite Complet de l'anatomie de l'homme was published so it is highly unlikely that this was an influence

---

[53] Kemp and Wallace, pp. 121-123.
[54] Amirault, p. 63.
[55] Amirault, p. 63.

on the work in question.⁵⁶ It is safe to say that these subtle stylisations were simply an artistic choice that were used to make the image more precise and legible. Nonetheless, Bourgery's use of striking visuals and simplification in his diagrams give them a balance between clarity and intricacy that could not be matched by the photography, where accuracy often made the images inscrutable. ⁵⁷

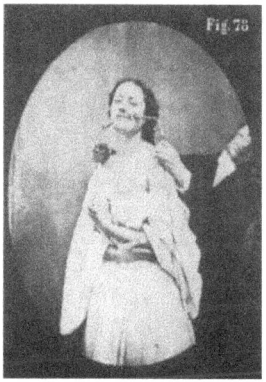

Fig. 15, Guillaume-Benjamin-Amand Duchenne, *A Scene of Coquetry*, Photograph, 1862.

---

⁵⁶ David Tomas, Beyond the Image Machine : A History of Visual Technologies (London, Bloomsbury Publishing Plc, 2004) P. 21.
⁵⁷ Amirault, pp. 55-56.

The move towards clarity and simplicity during this period also resulted in the culmination of the living anatomical figure in medical art. These figures, posed in a lifelike state, and stood as the moral, theological, and philosophical representatives of the medical text.[58] They were intended to demonstrate not only the artistic prowess of the medical artist, but the cultural importance of the text and the intelligence of it's author.[59] Yet, as artistically engaging as these works are, they failed to embody the practicality and consistency that was needed to ensure scientific accuracy and clear communication that was being demanded from medical art.[60] Thus images became naturalised and simplified, any posing was largely discouraged, except the purpose of clarity and illustration of various perspectives and angles. While Bourgery's figures adopted the pallor and appearance of still living people, their poses were either

---

[58] L. H. Wells, pp. 468-470.

[59] Martin Kemp, "Style and Non-Style in Anatomical Illustration: From Renaissance Humanism to Henry Grey", Journal of Anatomy, (Vol 216, No 2, February 2010) pp. 200-201.

[60] Kemp and Wallace, pp. 44-46.

highly simplified cross sections, or realistically based on the posing of a cadaver.[61] Even these minor cosmetic changes were falling out of favour due to being considered inaccurate and untrustworthy.[62] While this approach had been used by botanical and scientific artists for quite some time, it was the first major movement towards the use of medical diagrams as we know them today.[63]

---

[61] Hansen and Porter, p. 61.
[62] Kemp and Wallace, pp. 44-46.
[63] Hansen and Porter, p. 101.

The Aesthetics and Conventions of Medical Art

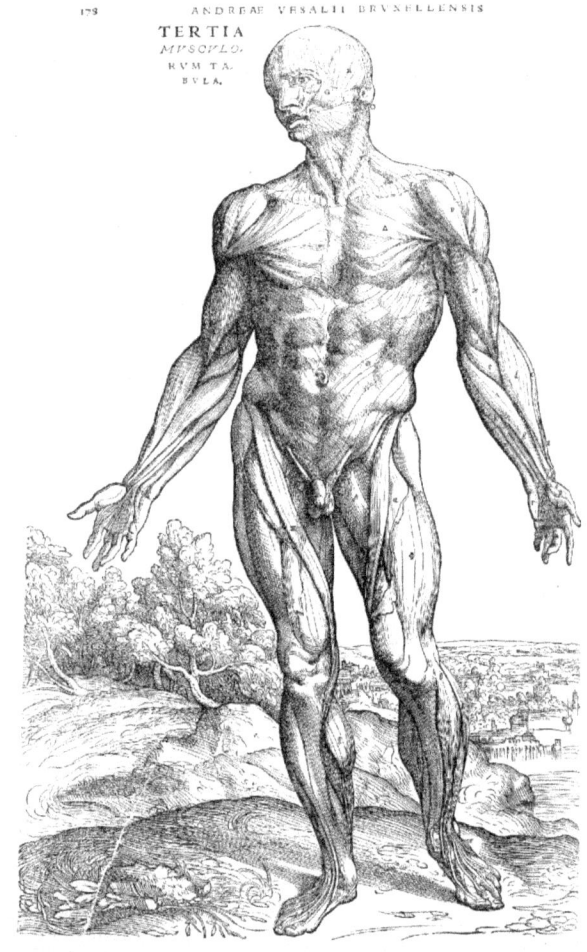

Fig. 16, Andreas Vesalius, *Ecorche*, Woodblock print, 1543.

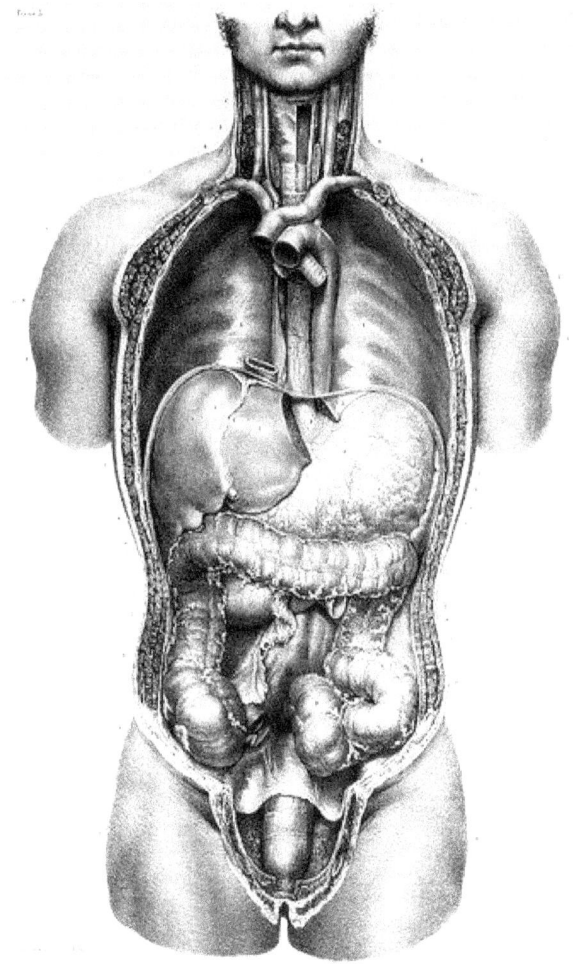

Fig. 17, Jean Baptiste Marc Bourgery,
Internal Organs, Lithographic print, 1854.

The Aesthetics and Conventions of Medical Art

As Medical science became more diverse and expansive and the information needed to constitute a full and complete understanding of the human body reached ever more complicated depths, the need for effective visual communication became tantamount to the effective use of medical art. As a result, medical artists in the 19th century contended with the need for stylisation against the ability to create art that was more accurate and realistic than ever before. In this chapter I examined how Bourgery's art attempted to reconcile these two styles and made them work in tandem to create richly detailed work that had the focus and precision to combine accuracy with a subtle reinterpretation of the body that effectively used minimalist stylings as an illustrative tool that clarified and streamlined the medical image. This style would be key to developing the artistic techniques needed to create images based on microscopic and abstract medical theory that would become increasingly important over the next century. Bourgery's use of stylised images also exemplified the movement toward the simplified, diagrammatic style of medical art that would become the blueprint for modern medical art practice, with creative interpretation of the figure being key to how we communicate and represent complex scientific fact. As time went on and the process of simplification and stylisation became more and more pronounced we can still see how small details and the use of texture play a role in how we register and understand medical art in its modern context.

The Aesthetics and Conventions of Medical Art

Chapter Three

Contemporary Medical Art

Modern medical art is largely defined by the rapid and unending state of innovation, changing constantly to suit a diverse set of practices ranging across the physical and theoretical. The style of art used to describe the interactions between disease and white blood cells will have little in common with an instructional diagram on laser eye surgery. Yet both rely on a visual language that is largely unacknowledged in both the importance of its role in medical understanding and the issues that any form of communication can be subject to, such as over reliance on a presumed base of knowledge, discriminatory visual biases, and a lack of practical application. One of the most pressing examples of these issues is the discriminatory/absent depictions of female, disabled and non-white bodies.[64] The lack of discourse and interrogation of contemporary medical art consistently causes issues in the quality of care available to those who were not included in this visual language as well as alienating patients and those looking to inform themselves on medical issues.

For the purposes of covering both the diverse array of practices and responses to the complex demands of modern scientific understanding as well as discussing the issues facing contemporary medical artists I have chosen to focus this chapter on the practice of Christine Borland, who has often focused her practice on the critique of medical art as both a source of alienation and the means by which we can understand ourselves.[65] Borland's art reflects on the distancing between modern medicine and its compromising

---

[64] Martin Kemp and Marina Wallace, <u>Spectacular Bodies: The Art and Science of the Human Body from Leonardo to Now.</u> (London, Hayward Gallery and University of California Press, 2000) pp. 150-156.

[65] Colin Martin, " Review: The Art of Being Human. Reviewed Work: Cast From Nature by Christine Borland", <u>British Medical Journal</u> (Vol. 342, No. 7810, June 2011) p. 1313.

past, as well as trying to reconstruct and understand how discoveries are being made in the present. The discomfort surrounding trial and error are key to her work and vital to understanding the shifting landscape of modern medical art. As I am not an expert in any of the medical fields being discussed I shall be endeavouring to balance trust on the basis of these representations and questioning the approach to their visual representation. Scientific objectivity is in many ways the understanding of how little we know, and in an age where we are constantly made aware of the ignorance of the past it is vital to acknowledge the ignorance of the present.

Contemporary medical art exists in an unusual space between the scientific and artistic application of imagery. While practical application is always a priority, many of the pieces that medical artists produce are considered aesthetically pleasing and have crossed the boundary between medical and gallery spaces. For the sake of comparison I will be discussing medical art in the context of work that is exploring new ways to represent the anatomical in an artistic manner. Vesalius and Bourgery's work was primarily focused on development and innovation rather than practicality on immediate application of the techniques they were pioneering, a suitable comparison would be the work of contemporary artists in the gallery. The focus on visual innovation and experimentation as well as the public facing nature of their work are more suitable modes of comparison than the work of medical artists.

The contemporary practice of medical art is primarily driven by technology, whether this is in the form of photography, 3d rendering, or digital printing. Increasingly these styles of visual representation are presented together in medical texts to illustrate a holistic overview of the concepts in question, with one widespread example of this practice being the combined use of digital rendering and photographs in visualising the subcutaneous effects of skin diseases.[66] This use of combining illustrative techniques

---

[66] Liam J. Caffery, David Clunie, Clara Curiel-Lewandrowski, Josep Malvehy, H. Peter Soyer, and Allan C. Halpern, "Transforming

began with the combined use of illustrations and photography in medical texts, with the illustrations being used to compensate for the lack of visual clarity in photographs due to both the quality of the photographs and the printing standards available up until the last 40 years.[67] It is only with the increased availability of digital access that such a range of imagery has been readily available to practitioners, since online journals and documents are free to distribute once they have been published. This widespread availability has led to a vast expansion of illustrative techniques, such as the use of ultrasound, CT scanning, and MRI all of which utilise soft tissue resistance to create a negative image that illustrates internal structures but each with different visual qualities and practical uses.[68]

---

dermatologic Imaging for the Digital Era: Metadata and Standards" Journal of Digital Imaging, (Vol. 31, No. 4, August 2018) p. 568.

[67] Andrew Paul Gardner, "Medical Diagnostic Imaging" in Michael R Peres's The Focal Encyclopedia of Photography : Digital Imaging, Theory and Applications, History, and Science, (New York, Taylor and Francis Group, 2007), pp. 563-568.

[68] William G. Bradley, "History of Medical Imaging", Proceedings of the American Philosophical Society, (Vol. 152, No. 3, September 2008) pp. 349-352.

Borland pushed this use of technology as a means of recreating intact complex biological structures in *'Cast From Nature'*, a series of sculptures inspired by the anonymity of personal nature of 3d anatomical records as can be seen in Fig 18. Borland created this piece based on a sculpture of a flayed man by John Goodsir in 1985. Intrigued by the anonymity of the subject who is depicted in such a vulnerable and visceral state Borland attempted to learn the identity of the person and created a series of restored plaster casts of the original piece, inverting them to place the focus of the figure as a moving person rather than a subject on an operating table.

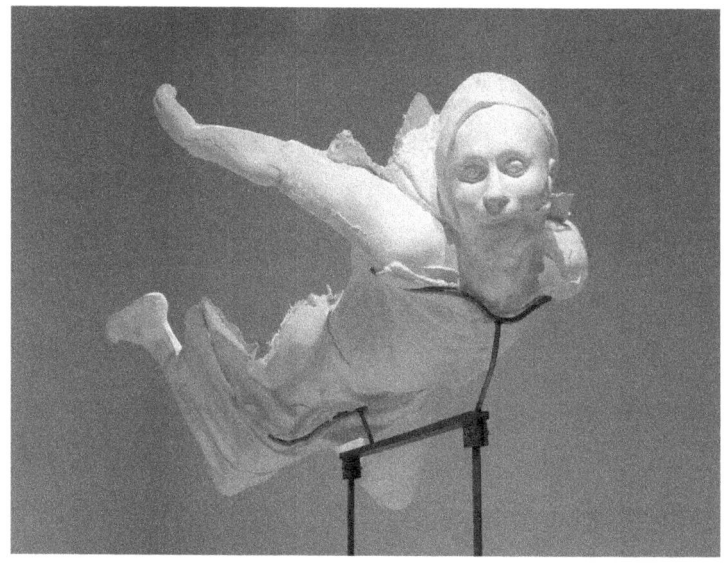

Fig. 18, Christine Borland, *Cast From Nature*, Plaster, 2011.

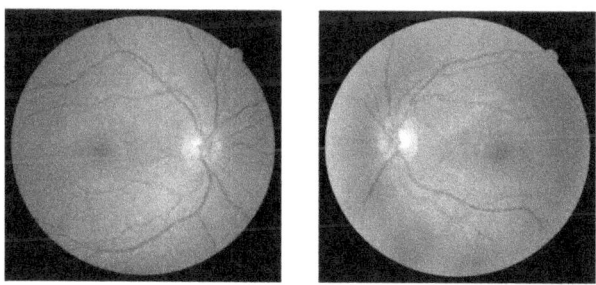

Fig. 19, N/A, Scan of the Authors Eyes, Optical Coherence Technology, 2022.

The use of technology has also allowed medical art to re-enter 3d space in force for the first time since the decline of the wax model of the 18th and 19th centuries.[69] 3d digital renders swiftly became a staple of the medical art industry after their introduction in the 1990's, as they offered a cost efficient, consistent reproduction of both internal structures and animated movement.[70] The use of these digital models has expanded with the introduction of 3d printing in recent years, as both have become ingrained in medical training, particularly in training surgeons as they offer a clear, animated insight into surgical techniques.[71] While this technique may seem like the perfect teaching tool, giving the observer an insight into both the structure and movement of surgical procedures, the cleanliness and lack of visceral

---

[69] Kemp and Wallace, p. 59
[70] Frank M. Corl, Melissa R. Garland, Elliot K. Fishman, "Role of Computer Technology in Medical Illustration", American Journal of Roentgenology, (Vol. 175, No. 6, 2000) pp.1519-1524.
[71] Matthew Hackett and Michael Proctor, "Three-Dimensional Display Technologies for Anatomical Education: A Literature Review", Journal of Science Education and Technology, (Vol. 24, No. 4, August 2016) p. 641.

realism of these images renders them a poor substitute for clinical observation.[72] While surgeons will obviously be observing the practices in person, others may be left with an inaccurate impression of the reality of these images.[73]

While a diagram or a drawing is obviously conceptualised as an artistic interpretation, all too often dimensionality can be mistaken for realism, especially where technology is involved. As research methods and modes of visual representation have expanded and evolved over recent years there has been an increasing pressure on medical artists to adapt their work to the strengths and abilities of technology rather than the needs of the patient or practitioner.[74] While many of the innovative technological practices that medical artists have both championed and utilised in their craft have

---

[72] Justine Garcia, ZhiLin Yang, Rosaire Mongrain, Richard L Leask, Kevin Lachapelle, "3D printing materials and their use in medical education: a review of current technology and trends for the future", BMJ Simulation and Technology Enhanced Learning, (Vol. 4, 2018) pp. 27-28.

[73] Joyce, pp. 257-258.

[74] Catherine Waldby, The Visible Human Project : Informatic Bodies and Posthuman Medicine (London, Taylor & Francis Group, 2000) pp. 98-99.

been excellent tools for discovery and communication, the pressure to be on the forefront of innovation has led to many conflicts of interest in their approach to visual communication. Oversimplifying diagrams so that they are cheaper to print, using stock models for 3d rendering, and the use of confidential patient photographs in medical texts have all been major issues in an industry where accuracy and visual quality are an ethical necessity.[75] Borland discussed this ethical quandary in her piece '*Did I request thee, Maker, From my clay to mould me man? Did I solicit Thee from Darkness to promote me?*', where she presented two copies of Mary Shelley's '*The Modern Prometheus*' printed using a poor quality photocopier.[76] The piece calls into question our over reliance on technology and the consequences of what will happen when we assume something will work despite a lack of evidence to the fact.

---

[75] I Berle, "Clinical photography and patient rights: the need for orthopraxy" Journal of Medical Ethics (Vol. 34, No. 2, February 2008) p. 89.
[76] David Barrett, "Review: Christine Borland", Frieze (7th June 1997) See: https://www.frieze.com/article/christine-borland-0.

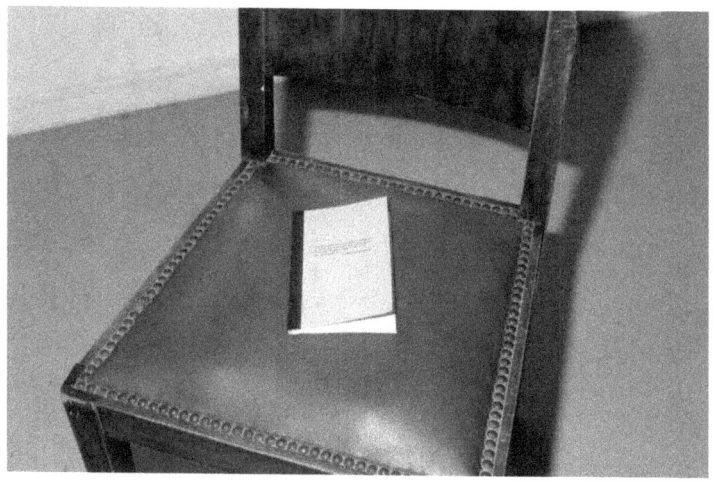

Fig, 20. Christine Borland, *Did I Request Thee, Maker, From my Clay to Mould Me Man? Did I Solicit Thee From Darkness to Promote Me?*, Ink on Paper, 1997.

As medical art has grown more specific and focused more on the functions and internal systems of the body, it has largely abandoned the representation of an existing person, instead relying on a simple, stylised model. This has been both a time-saving and privacy based development in medical art as the focus on 3d rendering, stylisation of medical diagrams, and the improvements to patient rights and patient privacy have all pushed this standard of anonymity in the medical figure.[77] The inclusion of a person's face and body have become an active choice in medical art rather than simply an expected quality which is excellent in terms of the aforementioned standards, but has presented issues in other areas of medical art as it became the accepted norm. The obvious issue with this stylistic practice is the dehumanisation of patients and the illusion of a neutral body.[78] One of the most egregious examples of these issues is the fact that up until very recently dermatological imaging which rarely accounted for how skin tone would affect the presentation of visual symptoms on darker skin tones and used pale skin as the default example.[79] The lack of reflective analysis on who they were representing

---

[77] I Berle, pp.90-91.
[78] Rebecca Gowland, Tim Thompson, Human Identity and Identification (Cambridge, Cambridge University Press, 2013), pp. 16-36
[79] J.C. Lester, J.L. Jia, L. Zhang, G.A. Okoye, E. Linos, "Absence of images of skin of colour in publications of COVID-19 skin manifestations", British Journal of Dermatology (Vol. 183, No. 3, September 2020) p. 593.

in these photographs caused issues with diagnosis and quality of care across a spectrum of medical issues.

The continued myth of the 'neutral' body as representational norm, which I touched on previously, is based on the idea that any human figure can represent a physical norm in medical art. These thin, able-bodied, caucasian figures being presented as the baseline for a normal, healthy body has had a major effect on the quality of information and quality of medical care for those who do not resemble these models. Not only in terms of discriminatory behaviour but also in professional understanding of different bodies and design of medical devices.[80] This has had a major impact on fat and disabled people whose bodies are consistently treated as outliers in the field of medical art, leading to a widespread lack of understanding on how various body structures can affect

---

[80] Claudia Wallis , "Fixing Medical Devices That Are Biased against Race or Gender" Scientific American, (1 June 2021) See: https://www.scientificamerican.com/article/fixing-medical-devices-that-are-biased-against-race-or-gender/.

how the body works.[81] Yet, while this is widely understood to be an issue of discrimination, the pervasive idea of a separation between these neutral figures and the reflection of artistic interpretation has made the subject difficult to tackle. Borland discussed this issue in the *'From Life Project'*, where she exhibited a reconstructed human skeleton across a series of slides alongside a series of diamonds that have been mounted on the heads of nails and driven into the floor.[82] The work reflects not only the value that we put on artificial reconstructions but the distance that we put between ourselves and the medical model, where reconstructed bones are photographed and those photographs projected, leaving neither the physicality of the reconstruction nor the physical surface of the photographs. The person who once lived and breathed, who is the basis of all this material is lost amongst the movements and shifts

---

[81] April Herndon, "Disparate but Disabled: Fat Embodiment and Disability Studies" NWSA Journal, (Vol. 14, No. 3, 2002) pp. 125-126.
[82] Barrett, See: https://www.frieze.com/article/christine-borland-0.

that it took to both conceal and represent their physical form.

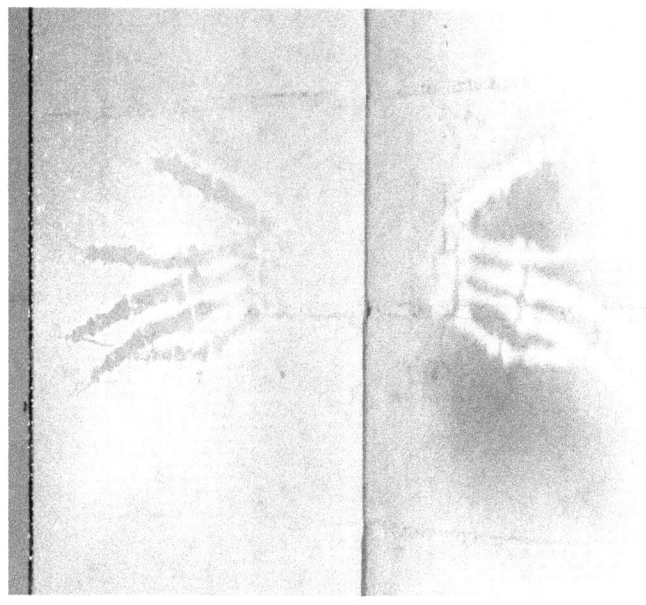

Fig. 21, Christine Borland, *From Life*, Mixed Media, 1994-1997.

The Aesthetics and Conventions of Medical Art

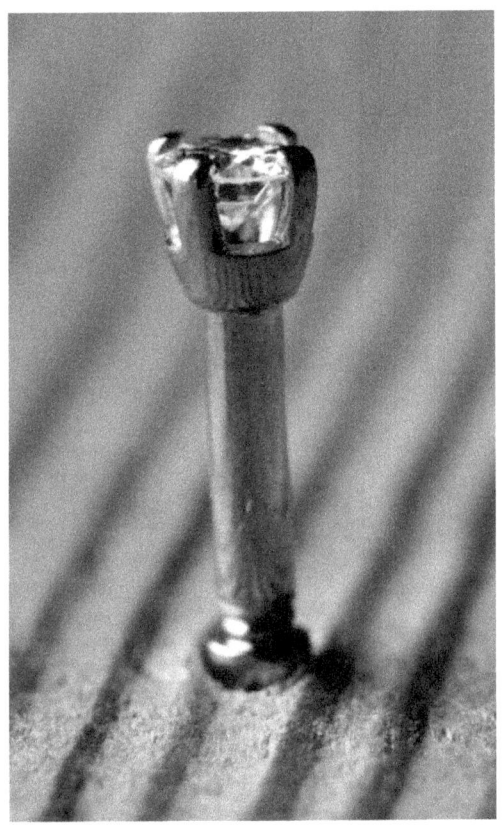

Fig. 22, Christine Borland, *From Life*, Mixed Media, 1994-1997.

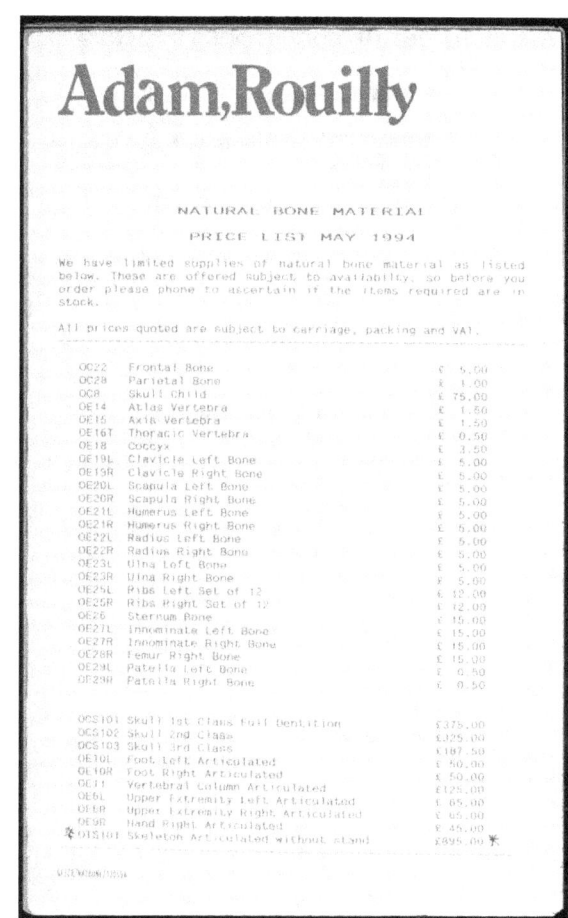

Fig. 23, Christine Borland, *From Life*, Mixed Media, 1994-1997.

The abstract nature of contemporary medical art is not simply a matter of practicality and patient privacy, it is also utilised as a communication tool for the vast array of theoretical and microscopic disciplines and studies that have become increasingly important over the past century.[83] Santiago Ramón y Cajal's pencil and ink drawings, documenting the first developments in modern neuroscience largely set the stage for this style, as Cajal recorded his findings with a focus of proportional accuracy and a simplified style.[84] Many of his drawings blended interpretation with observation, such as *'Celula del lobulo cerebral electrico del torpedo'*, which simplified the figure while utilising details the the edge of his microscope to create a box of information.[85] Rendering the information outside of

---

[83] George Weisz, Divide and Conquer : A Comparative History of Medical Specialization (Oxford, Oxford University Press, 2006) pp.87-89.
[84] William H. F. Addison, "Santiago Ramón Y Cajal" The Scientific Monthly (Vol. 39, No. 6, December 1934) p. 569.
[85] Roberta Smith, "A Deep Dive Into the Brain, Hand-Drawn by the Father of Neuroscience" The New York Times, (18 January 2018) See:

the cell in question would have been distracting, and would not have failed to provide a visual context due to the microscopic nature of the subject and as such the fervent realism of earlier medical art becomes antithetical to adequate visual communication. This style of microscopic representation has blossomed in contemporary medical art with artists such as Ella Maru, an illustrator who works in the more traditional form of medical art of providing images to academic texts to help illustrate medical theory as well as practice. As seen in Fig. 26, *Bacterial hairs power nature's electric grid*, her work draws on the use of bold simplistic shapes and dimensionality to depict complex internal structure on a microscopic level.[86]

---

https://www.nytimes.com/2018/01/18/arts/design/brain-neuroscience-santiago-ramon-y-cajal-grey-gallery.html.

[86] Rachel Walker, "The Path of a Scientific Illustrator: An Interview with Ella Marushchenko", <u>University of Rochester Career Story Q&A seminar Series</u> (7 October 2016)
See:https://www.urmc.rochester.edu/education/graduate/ur-best-blog/october-2016/the-path-of-a-scientific-illustrator-an-interview.aspx

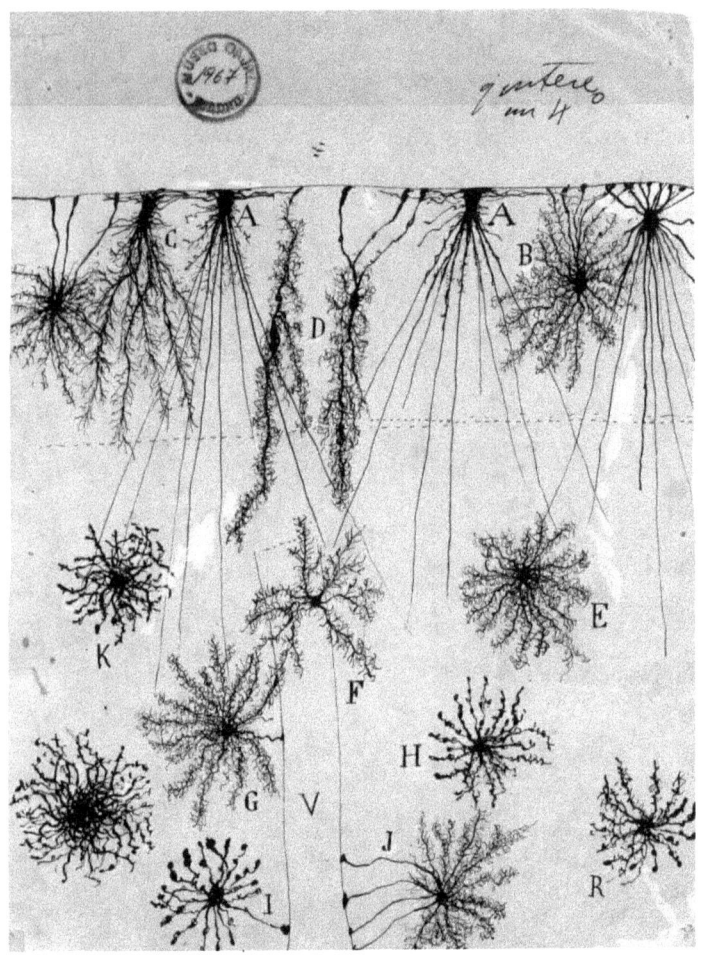

Fig. 24, Santiago Ramón y Cajal,
Glial cells of the cerebral cortex of a child, Ink on Paper, 1904.

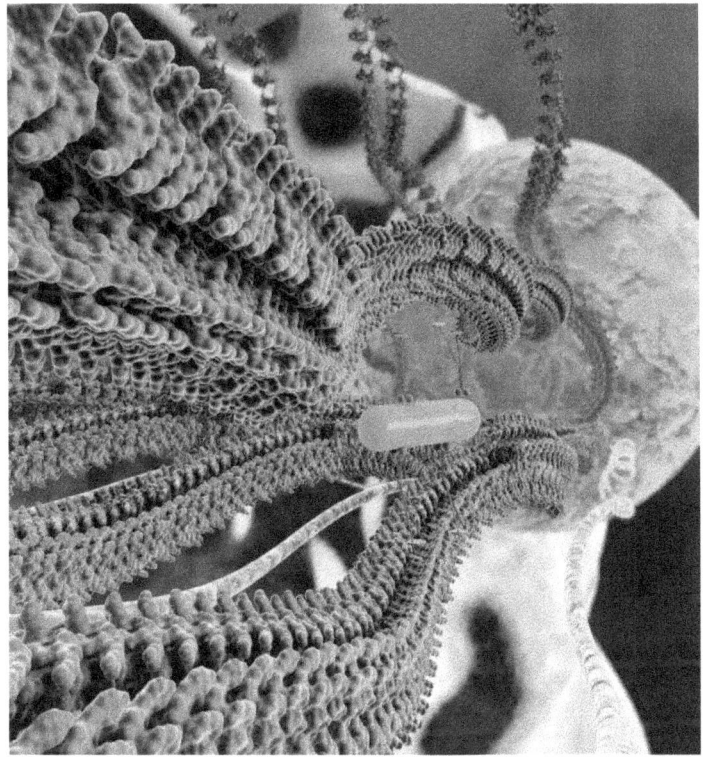

Fig. 25, Ella Maru Studio, *Kinesins are ATP-dependent motor proteins that can generate force and displacement along microtubules*, Digital Render, 2018.

The simple, graphic style that has become synonymous with contemporary medical art has also been driven by the saturation of imagery in medicine, and particularly in medical training. Crafting images that are easy to remember and can be paired with extensive text without becoming overly complicated is one of the key components of medical art practice. This methodology does make one question - if these works with their simplistic, direct style of communication will retain their legibility over time will they become documents of knowledge or simply the means by which it was once communicated? Christine Borland's work has often faced this very criticism, as critics emphasised the need for context and prior research to understand her concepts and methodologies. One poignant example of the elusiveness of context in her work can be seen in her sculptural piece *"Bullet Proof Breath"*, where she recreated the bronchi of the human lung and wrapped it in strings of spider silk. The piece was inspired by the experimental use of orb-weaver spider silk as a bullet proof material but without that context there is a disconnect between author intentions and audience understanding that is celebrated in traditional art circles but presents a source of concern when the work is made with practical communication in mind.

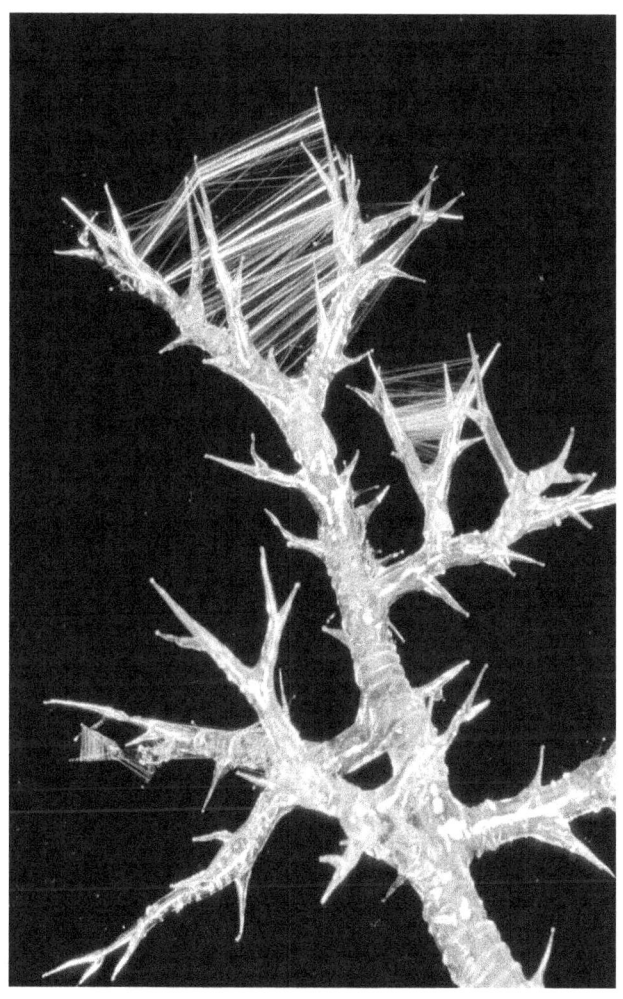

Fig. 26, Christine Borland, *Bullet Proof Breath*, Glass and Spider Silk, 2001.

The Aesthetics and Conventions of Medical Art

As information is continually pushed as a constantly updating, replaceable commodity, are artists being pushed to treat their work as perishable? As each diagram and render is treated as a stepping stone that will inevitably be replaced and improved, the act of creating them becomes open to experimentation and development. Adapting increasing complex theories and information into a visual format has become an essential aspect of both education and research, stylisation and simplicity is key to adapting information for consumption and widespread understanding. However, this practice can fail to account for the complex nature of medicine, as well as the plethora of experiences that need to be taken into account when approaching the human body. Putting aside the consumptive nature of medical illustration and reflecting on the importance that these images have in the lives of both patients and practitioners is key to understanding the rift between human needs and industry standards that can impact on the efficacy and reception of the work. Yet even as these issues present themselves, the work of medical artists continues to the development and distribution of medical knowledge in both the public and professional spheres.

The Aesthetics and Conventions of Medical Art

Ellen Harrold

Conclusion

Contemporary medical art is an international practice built on an ideal of giving people and practitioners an understandable reference point in their understanding of the human body. Due to the extensive representation of medical art in people's recognition of biology and the human body, the contemporary canon of medical art can seem both ubiquitous and logical. The prevailing belief amongst both professionals and the wider public seems to be that our understanding of medical art has reached an inevitable destination based on what is most accessible and efficient. However, analysing the history and development of medical art seems to show the clear influence of religious and cultural interpretations of the human body, as well as many instances of artistic licence in the technical development of medical art. I wish to explore if and how these artistic practices and interpretations of medicine and anatomy have survived and adapted to the scrutiny and demands of contemporary medical art. Vast technological advances may have improved our ability to visualise and deconstruct the most minute and delicate parts of human anatomy but has the reconstruction and communication of these processes evolved to the same degree? We can analyse the capillaries on our eyes down to the cells and atoms that make up the base of their structure but the line we use in their visual description remains the same as before. The intersection between art, culture, science and the perception of the human body as subject matter are inextricably linked to our understanding of the physical self. Accepting any representation as fact seems diminutive to the complexity of physical form, so to understand and analyse how we perceive and display the mechanisms of the self plays a vital role in expanding the artistic development that follows.

Contextualising the ethos and stylistic narrative that began modern medical art is key to understanding how it may progress as there has been very little challenge to our understanding of medical depictions in recent history. Given

Ellen Harrold

the current climate surrounding medical art, with large changes being made in our understanding of the human body through rapid scientific innovation, technological advances, and large-scale social movements I focused my research on periods that would reflect these conditions. Based on my research I chose to focus my analysis on the work of Andreas Vesalius and the cultural influences of the Renaissance and the work of Jean-Baptiste Marc Bourgery and the Industrial Revolution. Based on historical and artistic analysis of the works produced during these time periods I discussed current patterns and how they reflect and evolve from the work of the past. From here I focused on the practice of contemporary medical art, and its place as both a fine art practice and a form of scientific illustration, focusing on the work of Christine Borland, whose work has drawn on both scientific and artistic influences to create medical art for the gallery space.

For my first chapter I focused on the work of Vesalius and the introduction of medical art into popular print during the Renaissance. The tension between emerging scientific methodology and the traditions of the Christian church and the prevailing belief in Galenic medical theory created a tense atmosphere around the emerging art form. Many of the images produced during this period were reminiscent of popular art forms at the time, drawing on Christian and Greco-Roman influences and styles to evoke the prestige that would go on to attract wealthy patrons and collectors. This would set a precedent for centuries to come, as medical artists strove for physical attractiveness and intellectual stylings in their books to gain the approval of their peers and their patrons. The drive to craft perfectly accurate medical images that also integrated layers of symbolism showing the intellect of the author and artist created a bounty of fascinating art pieces. However, this approach was ineffective for developing the level of effective visual communication that we demand from the discipline today.

From the analysis of Vesalius and the influences of the Renaissance I moved onto Bourgery for my analysis of medical art during the Industrial Revolution for chapter 2. Unlike the first chapter which dealt with the emergence of an art form, the focus is on the beginning of the transitional period from the height of realism and aesthetic appeal to the much more utilitarian style that we associate with medical art today. Emerging theories on body chemistry and the importance of interconnected biological systems as well as the increasing demand for up to date information were major factors in this transition, with technological threats such as the camera speeding it along. Bourgery's work represents the culmination of the focus on aesthetics as an integral part of medical art as pragmatism and efficiency came to the forefront.

Chapter 3 was a primarily reflection on the challenges that medical art faces today. Without the luxury of historical perspective it is virtually impossible to predict which innovations and changes will take root and influence the future of medical art. Instead I directed my focus towards artistic responses to issues within medical art such as: discrimination, focus on output over quality, and the use of a homogenous style that doesn't reflect the needs of the practitioners and patients. I believe that looking at the artistic responses to these issues provide more insight into the progress and future of medical art that once could glean from experimental techniques or what is popular right now.

The aesthetics and techniques of medical art are consistently the result of artistic responses to culture, science and trends in the wider art market, drawing on imagery that connects information with understanding. Medical art doesn't appear to drive our understanding of the human body, instead it is shaped by it, Vesalius's religious references, Bourgery's focus on beauty, and Borland's holistic abstraction didn't emerge to show us how to see our bodies, they reflect how we understand ourselves and the interaction between our bodies and the world around us. One can safely ascertain that as long as our understanding and interpretation of the self and the world continues to evolve, so shall medical art.

From the dominant Christian themes and Greco-Roman influences of Andreas Vesalius to the diagrammatic style and vivid illustrative techniques of Jean-Baptiste Marc Bourgery, medical artists have left traces of themselves in their work.

Ellen Harrold

Much like the two aforementioned historical periods we are living in a period of rapid technological development and societal change that has placed an emphasis on production and constant updating of information that has led to an explosion of images. Where the woodblock and lithographic print stood in their time we now have computers, capable of producing images of a better quality and consistency than ever before. Contemporary practice has also fallen to the idea that our depiction of medicine and the human body represents a final evolution in the art form, having been perfected and taking its place as the permanent mode of representation. Yet with the context of history one can see that this is not true, our understanding of the body and our communication needs will continue to evolve and develop as time marches on. This does not negate the importance of these images as they will live on as historical and artistic work, documents of discovery and scientific development that will continue to inform future practices and guide medical artists for years to come.

The Aesthetics and Conventions of Medical Art

References

Addison, William H F. "Santiago Ramón Y Cajal" *The Scientific Monthly*. Vol 39:6, December 1934, pp. 567-570.

Amirault, Chris. "Posing the Subject of Early Medical Photography". *Discourse*, Vol 16: 2, 1993-94, pp. 51-76.

Barkan, Leonard, "The Beholder's Tale: Ancient Sculpture, Renaissance Narratives" *Representations*, Vol 44, Autumn 1993, pp. 133-166.

Barrett, David. "Review: Christine Borland". *Frieze*, 7th June 1997, https://www.frieze.com/article/christine-borland-0. Accessed: 8 November 2021.

Berle, I. "Clinical photography and patient rights: the need for orthopraxy" *Journal of Medical Ethics*. Vol 34:2, February 2008, pp. 89-92.

Bradley, William G. "History of Medical Imaging" *Proceedings of the American Philosophical Society*, Vol 152:3, September 2008, pp. 349-361.

Burgess, Jonathan S. The Death and Afterlife of Achilles. Baltimore, John Hopkins University Press, 2009.

Caffery, Liam J. Clunie, David. Curiel-Lewandrowski, Clara. Malvehy, Josep. Soyer, Peter H. Halpern, Allan C. "Transforming Dermatologic Imaging for the Digital Era: Metadata and Standards" *Journal of Digital Imaging*. Vol 31:4, August 2018, pp. 568-577.

Calcutt, John. "Review Christine Borland". *Map Magazine*, March 2007, https://mapmagazine.co.uk/christine-borland. Accessed 6th November 2021.

Catani, Marco. Sandrone, Stefano. Brain Renaissance : From Vesalius to Modern Neuroscience. Oxford, Oxford University Press, 2015.

Clark, Harry, "Foiling the Pirates: The Preparation and Publication of Andreas Vesalius's De Humani Corporis Fabrica" *The Library Quarterly: Information, Community, Policy*, Vol 51:3, 1981, pp. 301-311.

Cooper, Glen M. "Numbers, Prognosis, and Healing: Galen on Medical Theory" *Journal of the Washington Academy of Sciences,* Vol 90: 2, Summer 2004, pp. 45-60.

Corl, Frank M. Garland, Melissa R. Fishman, Elliot K. "Role of Computer Technology in Medical Illustration" *American Journal of Roentgenology*. Vol 175:6, 2000, pp. 1519-1524.

Craig, Tina. "Treasures of the Library No 15". *Royal College of Surgeons Bulletin*, Vol 81: 5, 1999.

Flamm, Eugene S. Pozeg, Zlatko L. "Vesalius and the 1543 Epitome of his "De humani corporis Fabrica librorum": A Uniquely Illuminated Copy" *The Papers of the Bibliographical Society of America,* Vo, 103:2, 2009, pp.199-220.

Furlong, Gillian. Treasures from UCL. UCL Press, 2015.

Ganso, Emil. Janson, H. W. "The Technique of Lithographic Printing". *Parnassus*, Vol 12: 7, November 1940, pp. 16-21.

Garcia, Justine. Yang, ZhiLin. Mongrain, Rosaire. Leask, Richard L. Lachapelle, Kevin. "3D printing materials and their use in medical education: a review of current technology and trends for the future" *BMJ Simulation and Technology Enhanced Learning.* Vol 4, 2018, pp. 27-40.

Garner, Andrew Paul. "Medical Diagnostic Imaging" in Michael R Pere's The Focal Encyclopedia of Photography : Digital Imaging, Theory and Applications, History, and Science. New York, Taylor and Francis Group, 2007.

Getz, Faye. Medicine in the English Middle Ages. New Jersey, Princeton University Press, 1998

Gowland, Rebecca. Thompson, Tim. Human Identity and Identification. Cambridge, Cambridge University Press, 2013.

Hackett, Matthew. Proctor, Michael. "Three-Dimensional Display Technologies for Anatomical Education: A Literature Review" *Journal of Science Education and Technology.* Vol 24:4, August 2016, pp. 641-654.

Hansen, Julie V. Porter, Suzanne. The Physician's Art: Representations of Art and Medicine. Durham, Duke University Library and Duke University Museum of Art, 1999

Harcourt, Glenn. "Andreas Vesalius and the Anatomy of Antique Sculpture" *Representations,* No 17, Special Issue: The Cultural Display of the Body, Winter 1987, pp. 28-61.

Herndon, April. "Disparate but Disabled: Fat Embodiment and Disability Studies" *NWSA Journal.* Vol 14:3, 2002, pp. 120-137.

Kemp, Martin. "Style and Non-Style in Anatomical Illustration: From Renaissance Humanism to Henry

Grey". *Journal of Anatomy*, Vol 216: 2, February 2010, pp. 192-208.

Kemp, Martin. Picturing Knowledge: Historical and Philosophical Problems Concerning the Use of Art in Science, Toronto, University of Toronto Press, 1996.

Kemp, Martin. Wallace, Marina. Spectacular Bodies: The Art and Science of the Human Body from Leonardo to Now. London, Hayward Gallery and University of California Press, 2000.

Kousser, Rachel. "Destruction and Memory on the Athenian Acropolis" *The Art Bulletin*, Vol 91:3, September 2009, pp. 263-282.

Laurenza, Domenico. "Art and Anatomy: Images from a Scientific Revolution" *The Metropolitan Museum of Art bulletin*, Vol 69:3, Winter 2012, pp. 4-48.

Lester, J C. Jia, J L. Zhang, L. Okoye, G A. Linos, E. "Absence of images of skin of colour in publications of COVID-19 skin manifestations" *British Journal of Dermatology*. Vol 183:3, September 2020, pp. 593-595.

Macaulay, David. "Review: The Body Skechers". *The Wilson Quarterly*, Vol 30: 4, Autumn 2006, p. 109-110.

MacLeod, Christine. "Strategies for Innovation: The Diffusion of New Technology in Nineteenth-Century British Industry". *The Economic History Review*, Vol 45: 2, May 1992, pp. 285-307.

Martin, Colin. "Review: The Art of Being Human. Reviewed Work: Cast From Nature by Christine Borland" *British Medical Journal*. Vol 342:7810, June 2011, p. 1313.

Martin, David L. Curious Visions of Modernity : Enchantment, Magic, and the Sacred. London, The MIT Press, 2011

Pantin, Isabelle. "Analogy and Difference: A Comparative Study of Medical and Astronomical Images in Books" in Nicholas Jardine and Isla Fay's (Ed.) Observing the World Through Images: Diagrams and Figures in the Early-Modern Arts and Sciences. Leiden, Brill. 2014

Park, Katherine. "The Criminal and the Saintly Body: Autopsy and Dissection in Renaissance Italy" *Renaissance Quarterly*, Vol 47:1, Spring 1994, pp. 1-33.

Parshall, Peter. "Introduction: The Modern Historiography of Early Printmaking" *Studies in the History of Art,* Vol 75, 2009, pp. 9-15.

Smith, Roberta. "A Deep Dive Into the Brain, Hand-Drawn by the Father of Neuroscience" *The New York Times.* 18th January 2018.

Stelmacowich, Cindy. "Bodies of Knowledge: The Nineteenth-Century Anatomical Atlas in the Spaces of Art and Science". *Canadian Art Review*, Vol 33: ½, 2008, pp.75-86.

Stelmacowich, Cindy. "The Art of Anatomical Science". *Canadian Medical Association Journal,* Vol 175: 5, 2006, pp. 505-506.

Tomas, David. Beyond the Image Machine : A History of Visual Technologies. London, Bloomsbury Publishing Plc, 2004.

Waldby, Catherine. The Visible Human Project : Informatic Bodies and Posthuman Medicine. London, Taylor & Francis Group, 2000.

Weisz, George. Divide and Conquer: A Comparative History of Medical specialisation. Oxford, Oxford University Press, 2006.

Wells, L. H. "The "Sabio" and "Sylvester" Families of Anatomical Fugitive Sheets: Note on a Pair of Sheets in the National Library of Medicine". *Bulletin of the History of Medicine*, Vol 40: 5, September 1966, pp. 467-475.

Williams, Brian. Cameron, Linda. "Images in health care: potential and problems". *Journal of Health Services Research & Policy*, Vol 14: 4, October 2009, pp. 251-254.

Wootton, David. Bad Medicine : Doctors Doing Harm since Hippocrates. Oxford, Oxford University Press, 2007.

Worboys, Michael. "Practice and the Science of Medicine in the Nineteenth Century". *Isis*, Vol 102: 1, March 2011, pp. 109-115

Acknowledgements

I would like to thank the staff of IADT for their guidance and encouragement, throughout my time there. I would also like to acknowledge my family and friends for their support. I give special mention to my cousin Kim and my grandmother Patsy, whose relentless pursuit of their passions have always, and will always carry me forward.

The Aesthetics and Conventions of Medical Art

Ellen Harrold

Artist's images:

Ellen Harrold

The Aesthetics and Conventions of Medical Art

Ellen Harrold

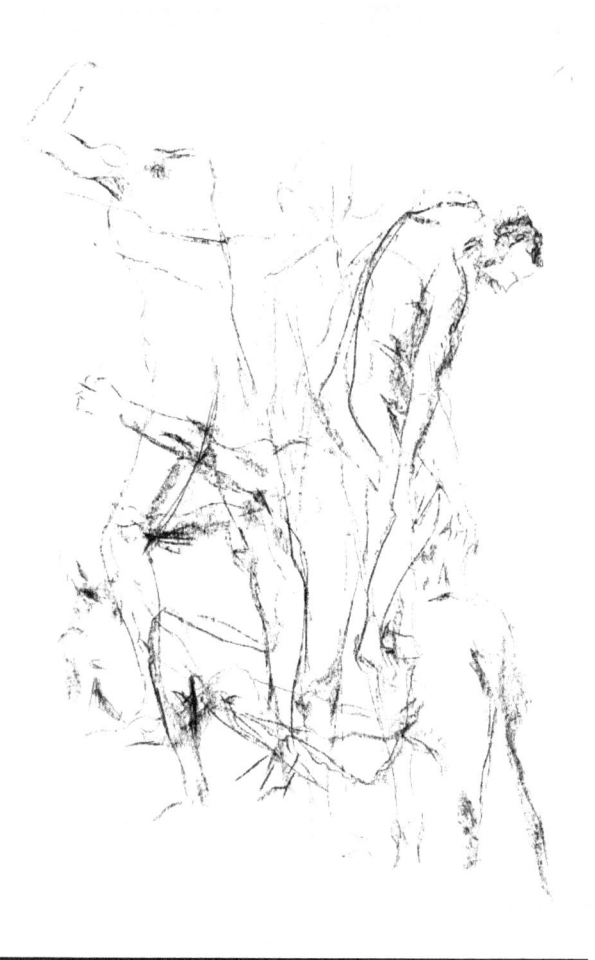

Fig. 28, Ellen Harrold, *Anatomical Studies*, Charcoal on Paper, 2022.

The Aesthetics and Conventions of Medical Art

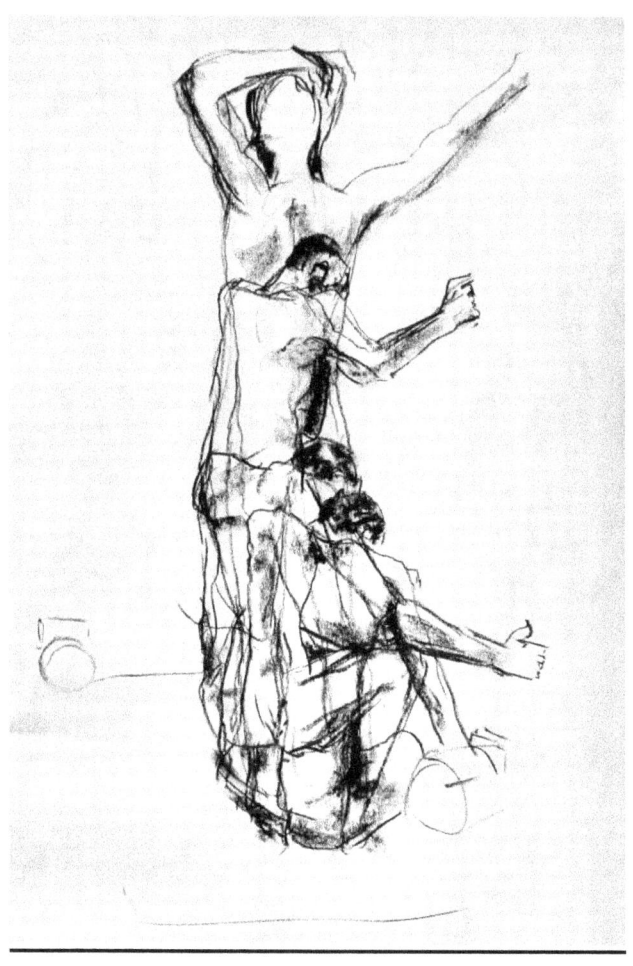

Fig. 29, Ellen Harrold, *Anatomical Studies*, Charcoal on Paper, 2022.

The Aesthetics and Conventions of Medical Art

Ellen Harrold

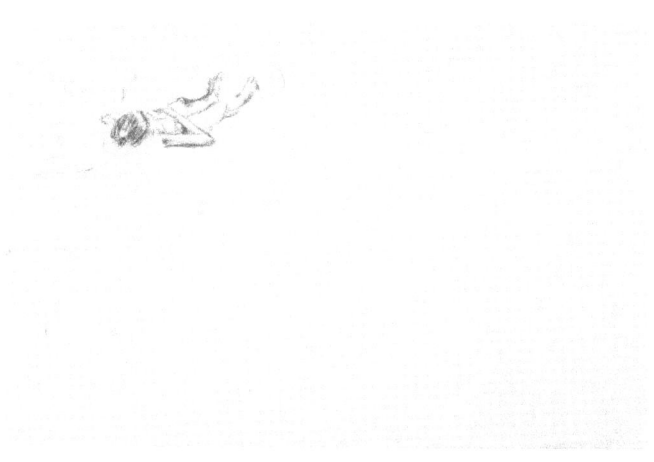

Fig. 30, Ellen Harrold, *Figure Rotation*, Pencil on Paper, 2022.

The Aesthetics and Conventions of Medical Art

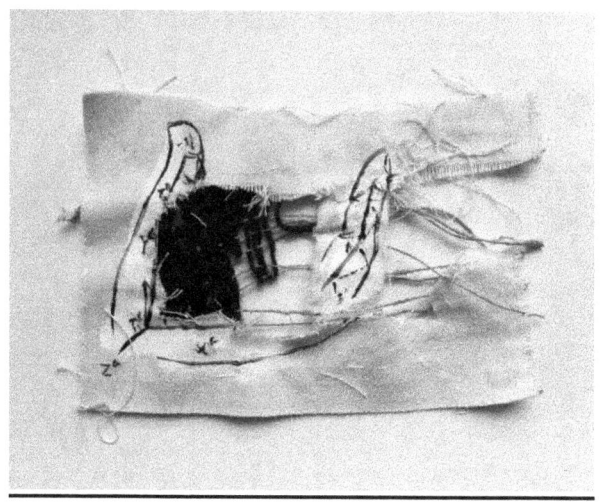

Fig. 31, Ellen Harrold, *Ligament Reconstruction*, Acrylic, Wool, and Nettle on Canvas, 2022.

The Aesthetics and Conventions of Medical Art

Ellen Harrold

BOOM!

This book was originally submitted as a dissertation in partial fulfilment of the requirements of a BA (Hons) in the Department of Art and Design at the Institute of Art, Design and Technology, Dun Laoghaire Faculty of Film, Art and Creative Technologies, Ireland.

The Aesthetics and Conventions of Medical Art

Ellen Harrold

A note about Boom Graduates

We propel graduates forward so they can make their mark on the world - we push the boundaries, share brilliant ideas and inspire possibility. We publish dissertations as books, presented gift-boxed at graduation ceremonies, delivering brand-new research to the world quicker than anyone else. We plant trees for every commissioned book sold, and give our Boom graduates the chance to profit-share from their brilliant ideas. Furthermore we donate the majority of our profits to funding research and scholarship for disadvantaged students who wouldn't normally be able to attend university. Through academic excellence and environmental sustainability, *Boom Graduates* are changing the world.

We are Boom Graduates - an imprint of Boom Publications Ltd. We are a more-than-profit company, dedicating over half our profits to providing university scholarships for underprivileged students across the world. We aim to become the globe's biggest provider of such scholarships – and if like Ellen, the author of this book, you'd also like to contribute to making the world a better place, please contact us: we publish monographs, edited books, and moreover our graduate series – Boom Graduates – are presented at graduation days across the world in archival, lined museum-quality presentation cases, engraved with the graduate's name and award.

Boom Publications are based at the Duncan of Jordanstone College of Art and Design, at the University of Dundee in Scotland. We were one of the winners of the 2022 Venture awards hosted by the Centre for Entrepreneurship, and have since been shortlisted for the Converge Challenge, a national award that brings together ambitious and creative thinkers with innovative ideas to work with industry experts to transform their ideas into sustainable companies operating in the commercial world. We are also climate conscious and work with agencies to plant a tree for each and every book commissioned, offsetting thousands of tonnes of carbon each year. Follow us on social media to watch our forest grow @boomgraduates.

Thank you for contributing by purchasing this book. Please visit our catalogues on www.boompublications.com.

The Aesthetics and Conventions of Medical Art

Ellen Harrold

Notes

The Aesthetics and Conventions of Medical Art

Ellen Harrold

The Aesthetics and Conventions of Medical Art

Ellen Harrold

The Aesthetics and Conventions of Medical Art

Ellen Harrold

www.ingramcontent.com/pod-product-compliance
Lightning Source LLC
Chambersburg PA
CBHW050007230526
45465CB00003BB/1298